Roman Conquests: The Danube Frontier

Roman Conquests: The Danube Frontier

Dr Michael Schmitz

Pen & Sword
MILITARY

First published in Great Britain in 2019 by
Pen & Sword Military
an imprint of
Pen & Sword Books Ltd
47 Church Street
Barnsley
South Yorkshire
S70 2AS

ISBN 978 1 84884 824 5

A CIP catalogue record for this book is available from the British Library.

Printed and bound in England
By TJ International Ltd, Padstow, Cornwall

Pen & Sword Books Ltd incorporates the Imprints of Pen & Sword
Aviation, Pen & Sword Family History, Pen & Sword Maritime,
Pen & Sword Military, Pen & Sword Discovery, Pen & Sword Politics,
Pen & Sword Atlas, Pen & Sword Archaeology, Wharncliffe Local History,
Wharncliffe True Crime, Wharncliffe Transport, Pen & Sword Select,
Pen & Sword Military Classics, Leo Cooper, The Praetorian Press, Claymore
Press, Remember When, Seaforth Publishing and Frontline Publishing.

For a complete list of Pen & Sword titles please contact
PEN & SWORD BOOKS LIMITED
47 Church Street, Barnsley, South Yorkshire, S70 2AS, England
E-mail: enquiries@pen-and-sword.co.uk
Website: www.pen-and-sword.co.uk

Dedication

I would like to dedicate this book to Bob Estrich. From the very beginning, when you took pity on a pair of poverty-stricken university students with a young baby and kept our computer running, to the end when you were helping us renovate our first house, a truer friend there hasn't been, I like to think this is the book you would have wanted me to write. A friend and lover of history lost too soon.

'What have the Romans ever done for us?'

Contents

List of Illustrations

Acknowledgements

Firstly, I would like to extend my most sincere thanks to Phil Sidnell, not only for the invitation to write this book but the patience he has shown the author through a very trying period. I would also like to thank my colleagues Professor Lynda Garland and Associate Professor Matthew Dillon, who have encouraged me throughout the process of writing, and Nigel Holman who selflessly gave up a number of relevant books. Finally, and most importantly, I would like to thank my partner Fiona, my sons Aidan and Cody and my daughter Isaboh for their support.

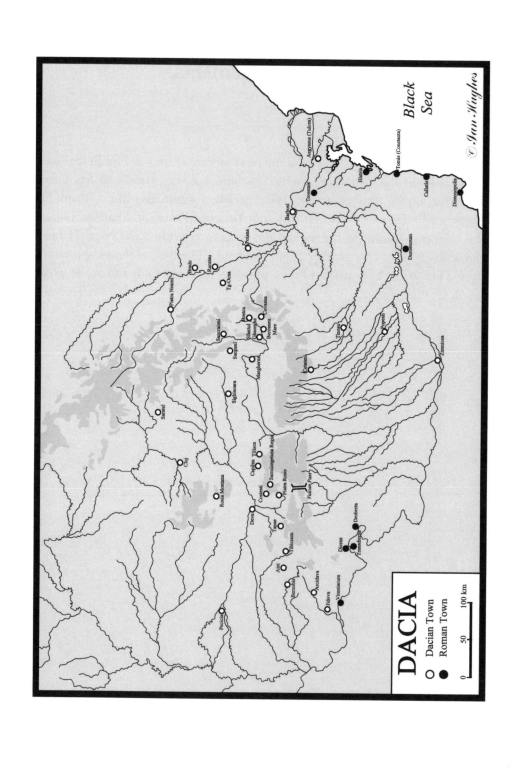

DACIA

○ Dacian Town
● Roman Town

Black Sea

0   50   100 km

© Ian Hughes

Aegyssus (Tulcea)
Troesmis
Barboşi
Histria
Tomis (Constanta)
Callatis
Dionysopolis
Durostorum
Tirgu
Buciumu
Tg.-Ocna
Piatra Neamt
Piroboridava
Sarmizegetusa
Breţcu
Sfântul Gheorghe
Covasna
Borosneu Mare
Comalau
Zimnicea
Tismana
Pojejena
Saratel
Sighisoara
Margineni
Saruni
Cluj
Roşia Montana
Cumidava Ulpica
Sarmizegetusa Regia
Deva
Comeşti
Piatra Rosie
Vulcan Pass
Tapae
Tibiscum
Drobeta
Azei
Berzobis
Acidava
Dierna
Tiansdierna
Micia
Vârmiacum
Pecinca

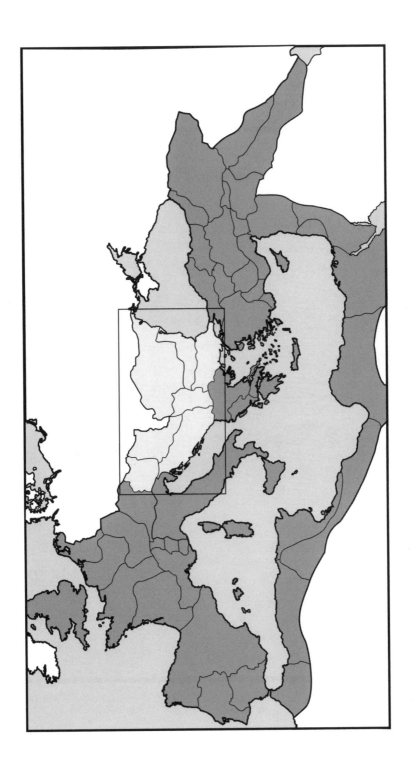

NORICUM

PANNONIA

ERAVISCI

ILLYRIA

0   100 km

Poetovio

Neviodunum

Andautonia

Siscia/Segesta

BREUCI

Metulum

Senia

Arupium

JAPODES

D A L M A T I A

DACIA

Singidunum

SCORDISCI

MOESIA

Salvium

DAESITIATES

Promona

DELMETAE

Delminium

Salona

Novae

Epidaurum

MACEDONIA

Pella

© John Hughes

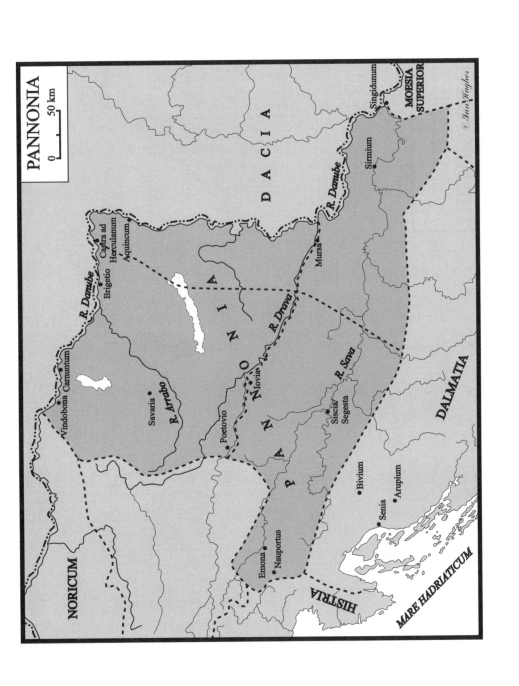

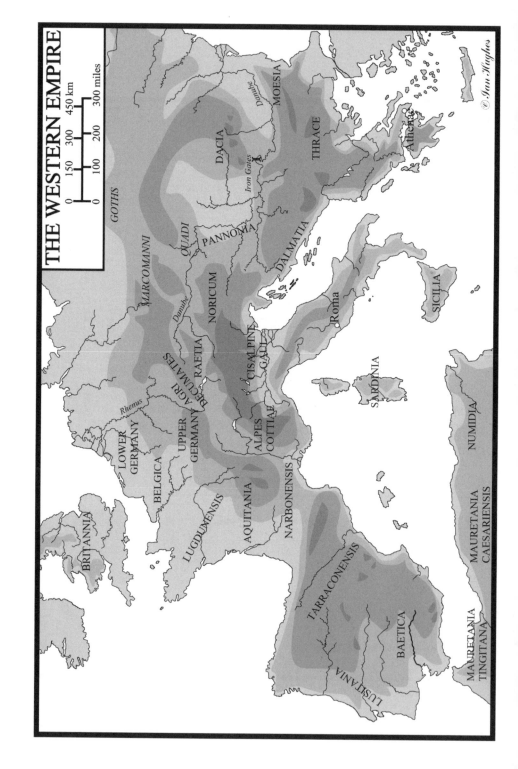

THE WESTERN EMPIRE

0   150   300   450 km
0   100   200   300 miles

© Ian Hughes

GOTHS

MARCOMANNI

QUADI

DACIA

Danube

MOESIA

Iron Gates

THRACE

Athenae

PANNONIA

NORICUM

DALMATIA

Danube

RAETIA

Roma

AGRI DECUMATES

CISALPINE GAUL

Rhenus

UPPER GERMANY

ALPES COTTIAE

SICILIA

LOWER GERMANY

BELGICA

SARDINIA

LUGDUNENSIS

AQUITANIA

NARBONENSIS

BRITANNIA

NUMIDIA

TARRACONENSIS

MAURETANIA CAESARIENSIS

LUSITANIA

BAETICA

MAURETANIA TINGITANA

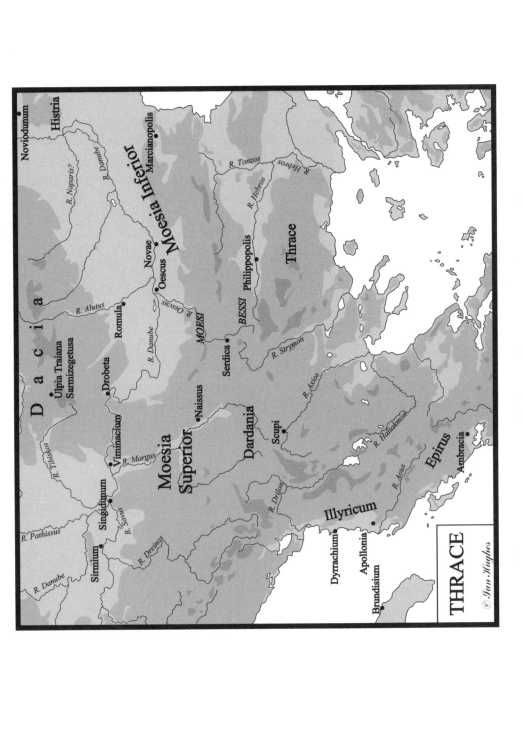

THRACE

© *Ian Hughes*

Introduction

The Danube frontier posed a continuous and serious threat to the Roman Empire from at least the time the first Roman general, Curio, reached the river in the 70s BC. This threat would last until the fall of the Empire more than five centuries later. It is clear that throughout this period the Romans had significant and frequent issues along this frontier and felt the need to conquer the people living along the Danube in order to maintain their own security and protect the important travel and communication links between the eastern and western parts of the Empire.

Roman conquests along this most volatile of frontiers occurred over a period of approximately 150 years and under the guidance of numerous emperors and generals, beginning with Octavian in 35 BC and ending with Trajan's conquest of Dacia in AD 107. Dacia, the last great Roman imperial acquisition, was also the first province to be surrendered. At its greatest extent the Danubian frontier formed the northern boundary of Raetia, Noricum, Pannonia, Moesia and the southern boundary of Dacia. It was the setting for numerous battles, important victories and significant Roman losses, costing many thousands of lives over the period examined. After Rome had completed its conquests along the Danube, the river formed the longest continuous natural border in continental Europe. This frontier, which stretched over 2,800km, was more than twice the length of the other major natural border in continental Europe, the Rhine. The Danube was therefore a justifiably important focus of Roman attention.

Rome faced many dangerous peoples in its wars along this frontier including Dalmatians, Pannonians, Germans, Sarmatians and Dacians, to name but a few. Rome's first military operation beyond the Adriatic, in 230 BC, brought the Romans into contact, for the first time, with the region of Illyricum. The Illyrians had caused Rome issues with their constant piracy on the Adriatic Sea, and perhaps more importantly still their apparent desire to expand along the coastline opposite Italy which threatened Roman security. In time Illyricum would be replaced by the Roman provinces of Illyricum, Dalmatia and Pannonia which fronted the Danube River. The first chapter examines this early contact and Rome's introduction to the region as this sets the scene for the conquests along the Danube that followed.

After a brief examination of Caesar's contact with the region, Octavian's conquests in Illyricum and the challenges he faced fighting the tribal peoples along the coast and into the mountainous regions of the hinterland will be examined. The young Octavian, at this time a triumvir and not yet the first emperor of Rome, conquered parts of Illyricum in the 30s BC, very nearly losing his life on campaign. The conquests of Raetia and Noricum, and Tiberius's continuation of Octavian's conquests in Illyricum, are the subject of the third chapter. Octavian, now Augustus, understanding the importance of a secure Danubian frontier, had devoted a significant part of his lifetime to securing the Danube region. Only five years before his death, Augustus was still directing affairs along the Danube, sending the future Emperor Tiberius to quash the extremely dangerous Pannonian rebellion (discussed in Chapter 4).

The best generals of their respective times were sent to the Danube to face Rome's enemies and maintain the integrity of this most important frontier. Marcus Agrippa, Tiberius, Trajan and Marcus Aurelius all spent significant time fighting along the Danube. The people they fought were seen by the Romans as being particularly warlike and dangerous from a very early period. The Romans took matters in this region seriously, as can be seen by the panic in Rome that often accompanied problems on this frontier. The emergence of a fledgling Dacian Empire posed a very significant threat to the Empire because of the unity this political construct entailed. A unified and technologically-advanced people on this frontier posed a new sort of threat. The Dacian people, with their brazen anti-Roman tendencies, attempts to form alliances with nearby neighbours and willingness to raid Roman territory, were a threat from the time of Julius Caesar but one that was not resolved until the reign of Trajan when the then-nascent Empire was crushed after two difficult and costly wars. The nature of Dacian unity is discussed in Chapter 5. The Flavian emperors on the Danube are discussed next with particular attention paid to Domitian's Dacian wars which were the precursors and to some degree the impetus to Trajan's wars (Chapter 7). The penultimate chapter focuses on Hadrian, Trajan's successor, the changing nature of imperialism and the increased fortification of the frontier. The Marcomannic wars that dominated the reign of Marcus Aurelius are the subject of the final chapter. These wars demonstrate that even though the Dacians had finally been conquered, other enemies were emerging on this frontier and external pressures were creating a situation that Rome would only be able to contain for so long.

The Danubian frontier has been relatively underrepresented in the modern literature, although this is starting to improve; there are of course a number of very good reasons for this including the difficulties associated with limited and sometimes contradictory source material that makes a detailed discussion almost impossible at times. Much of the region discussed in this book is also located in areas that have not been particularly accessible until relatively recently. This region was unquestionably of vital importance to the security of the Roman Empire. This frontier and the people on it and beyond it determined the limits of the Empire, contrary to the ambitions of a number of emperors who tried to extend beyond this river. Only one emperor managed to push beyond the Danube and hold territory, the last great conquering emperor, Trajan. The northern threat had been realized by the Romans early in their history and even though many attempts to neutralize this threat occurred none were able to end the threat in anything more than a temporary manner.

The Roman conquests along the Danube are an epic story stretching almost all the way across Europe. This region was inhabited by many warlike and numerous peoples and although Rome was able to master the Danube for a period of time, this frontier was amongst the most heavily garrisoned of all frontiers, demonstrating its importance to the Romans by the percentage of their overall military force that was posted here at any given time in order to keep the Empire safe.

Chapter 1

Illyricum: The Push Towards the Danube

This is a matter not to be lightly passed over, but deserving the serious attention of those who wish to gain a true view of the purpose of this work and of the formation and growth of the Roman Dominion.

Polybius, II.2.1

The First Illyrian War

It is the region of pre-Roman Illyricum and the first trans-Adriatic war of 230 BC that Polybius is referring to in the above passage. This war marked the beginning of Rome's contact with the people of the Danube and the inevitable Danubian conquests to follow.[1] Geographically, Illyricum at this time included three distinct areas: the Dalmatian coastline situated directly opposite the Italian peninsula, the Dinaric Alps which separate the coast from the hinterland and which can be crossed only via a few passes, and finally the Pannonian plains which directly bordered the Danube. Although no concerted effort was made to occupy and annex any of these regions until Octavian's Illyrian war between 35 and 33 BC, which is the subject of the next chapter, Roman contact began with the first trans-Adriatic war some 200 years earlier. Roman interests in the region of Illyricum were primarily sparked because of Rome's need to bring an end to the continued Illyrian piracy in the Adriatic. Rome saw the most powerful Illyrian king to date, with a larger navy and army than any previous Illyrian monarch, situated just across the Adriatic, which was too close for comfort. To make matters worse in the view of Rome, the Illyrian king Agron apparently had links with Demetrius of Macedon, another ruler in the region that Rome was not on good terms with.

The fact that the Illyrians were capable of and willing to expand along the Adriatic coastline made them a potential threat to Rome, and unquestionably to Roman shipping in the region.[2] Piracy was a major issue in the ancient world, particularly to nations such as Rome who were very heavily reliant on shipping for the delivery of staples such as wheat, and required serious attention.

Illyrian expansion along the Adriatic coastline began because Demetrius of Macedon had bribed the Agron to relieve the siege of the town of Medion.[3] The Aetolian League were attacking this town because they had tried to convince Medion's inhabitants to join their league, but because they had been rejected they sought to force these people to join them through military action, something Demetrius was opposed to.[4] Whilst the Aetolians were besieging the town, Agron sailed 100 boats at night, carrying a force of 5,000 Illyrians, down the Adriatic coastline to lift the siege.[5] The Illyrian vessels used by Agron's forces, known variously as lemboi, pinnaces or liburnians, were single-decked vessels apparently capable of carrying fifty troops each in addition to the oarsman required to row them.[6] They had a single bank of oars and were reputedly very fast and manoeuvrable. After engaging with the Illyrians, the Romans would adopt these vessels themselves. Apparently Octavian favoured them and used them against Antony and Cleopatra at the famous battle of Actium, his opponents preferring the more traditional heavier quinquereme. The Illyrian vessels might not have been able to withstand a head-on battle against the heavier warships but their real strength lay in their speed and manoeuvrability, as repeatedly demonstrated by the Illyrians.

Octavian's use of these vessels at the battle of Actium gives a clear indication of how they could be utilized against heavier opposition. It appears that the captains of Octavian's lemboi decided against using their rams to attack Antony and Cleopatra's fleet of larger ships as they were concerned that the lighter vessels would come off worse in a head-on engagement. Additionally, Antony's crews had been struck down by malaria which had resulted in many deaths leaving the vessels undermanned. Octavian's lighter vessels exploited their speed and manoeuvrability to sail at the heavier vessels, loose their missiles at the opposing crew and reverse course rapidly, moving out of the quinqueremes's range. The Macedonians also made use of this type of vessel, again not for open battle but rather to rapidly transport and land troops in strategically or tactically valuable positions. Additionally, it is clear that these fast light vessels were ideal for the national occupation of the Illyrians, piracy.[7] In both cases it was the troop-carrying capacity of these vessels that made them invaluable. This was further demonstrated when prior to the first Illyrian war, whilst the Illyrians were attacking Corcyra, a Greek force of ten warships was sent against them.[8] After a relatively indecisive action where seven regular warships belonging to the Illyrian's allies fought the Greek squadron, the Greek forces turned on the lighter Illyrian vessels in the hopes of crushing them. The Illyrians made inventive use of their lighter ships against the heavier Greek vessels, roping four of these vessels together and presenting their side to the oncoming Greek warships, inviting and allowing them to ram the lighter vessels.[9] The Greeks, much to their misfortune, took the bait and when the Greek vessels rammed the lashed-together Illyrians, the Greek warships became fouled and the Illyrian warriors, vastly outnumbering the hoplite contingents on board the Greek vessels, would board and capture them. On average a Greek warship would carry as few as fourteen hoplites and four archers, whereas each of the lighter Illyrian ships carried approximately fifty warriors.[10] As a result of the Illyrians' innovative tactics, the Greeks lost half of their ships.[11]

At Medion the Illyrian forces were well led. Having arrived during the night, they anchored as close to the town as was possible and landed their troops at daybreak. Immediately they formed into battle order and advanced on the Aetolian camp. Although surprised by the sudden appearance of the Illyrians, the Aetolians had sufficient time to form up, placing the bulk of their heavy infantry and cavalry on level ground near the camp and their light infantry and remaining cavalry at high points in front of their camp.[12] The Illyrian troops charged the light infantry and forced them from their positions largely due weight of numbers. This in turn compelled the cavalry that had been stationed with the light infantry to retreat, as failure to do so would have left them vulnerable to flank attacks by the Illyrian forces.[13] The retreating cavalry ran straight into the Aetolian heavy infantry on the plain, disrupting its formation.

Having taken the high ground, the Illyrians made use of this advantage against the Aetolian heavy infantry, rapidly routing the League's forces with the assistance of the Medionians who, upon seeing the Illyrian success, joined in the attack from the city.[14] Many of the Aetolians were killed and an even larger number were taken prisoner. The Illyrians captured all of the abandoned Aetolian arms and baggage, collecting as much booty as they could and immediately sailing home. Agron was so pleased with his victory against the Aetolian League that according to the sources he embarked on excessive celebrations which led to his death in just a matter of days.[15] This left his infant son Pinnes to succeed him on the throne. However, because of Pinnes's age his mother Teuta ruled in his name. It was with Teuta that the Romans were to go to war in 230 BC.

With Teuta as queen, Illyrian privateers were given permission to take any ship they came across. Furthermore, she assembled as large an army as her husband had and instructed her commanders that all countries should be treated as enemies.[16] Polybius's account is clearly biased by a misogynistic perspective common to the ancient authors and needs to be taken with a pinch of salt, particularly in his descriptions of the motivations of Queen Teuta. Polybius's suggestion that Teuta had no concept of the geo-political circumstances Illyria found itself in are perhaps a result of this bias. What is clear is that up until then the Romans had not interfered with Illyrian activities on their side of the Adriatic and it is quite likely that after Agron's successes Teuta felt that conquest of a larger proportion of the Adriatic coastline was a real and viable opportunity to expand Illyrian domination in the region.

In 230 BC the Illyrian forces laid siege to the island of Issa, which would provide the Romans with the excuse they needed to begin what became known as the First Illyrian War.[17] Unfortunately for Teuta, the rapid expansion of the Illyrians came to the attention of the Romans after the people of Issa sent an embassy to Rome requesting assistance. Although initially the Romans sent an embassy to investigate the situation, the murder of a Roman ambassador, seemingly on orders from the Illyrian queen, was what eventually convinced the Roman people to declare war.[18]

Interestingly enough, the Roman people were far from keen in becoming involved with the Illyrians, the plebians demonstrating this by initially voting against the war when the issue was raised by the Senate. At this time in Roman history, before the formation of the Empire, the Roman citizens who formed the *Comitia Centuriata* made the final decision as to whether or not Rome would go to war. Another war, not long after the conclusion of the First Punic War and when its privations were still being suffered, would not have been popular. It was only the death of the Roman envoy, who had been sent to determine what was happening at Issa, apparently on the orders of Teuta, and the argument that if they did not fight the Illyrians in their homeland then the Illyrians would likely attack them in Italy, that persuaded the plebians to vote in favour of military action against the Illyrians.[19]

229 BC saw the continuation of Illyrian aggression on the Adriatic coast, one contingent of Illyrian ships sailing to Epidamnus.[20] When asked what their purpose was by the local authorities, the Illyrians claimed that they were just stopping to resupply their ships. However, when they disembarked in order to collect water the Illyrians, having treacherously concealed weapons in their water jugs, surprised the guards assigned to protect the port and seized one of the city's towers, from where they were soon able to capture many of the walls around the town, and only after valiant resistance by the local inhabitants were the Illyrians eventually ejected from the city.[21] After this defeat, the Illyrian force made its way south to join with a second Illyrian contingent which had been sent further down the coast. This force, under the command of Demetrius of Pharos, had sailed through the Corcyran Straits and besieged the city of Corcyra.[22] The Corcyran and Illyrian forces engaged in an indecisive land battle resulting in the continuation of the siege, which eventually culminated with Corcyra's surrender to Demetrius. The Illyrians then returned to once again lay siege to Epidamnus.

It was at about this time the first force of Romans left Italy with its immediate goal being to lift the siege at Corcyra, but unfortunately the city had already been taken, which the Roman commanders only learned upon their arrival.[23] Fortunately for the Romans, however, it appears that Demetrius had had a falling-out with Queen Teuta and as a result was prepared to surrender Corcyra and Pharos to them.[24] In return the Romans made Demetrius a friend of the Roman people and he was allowed to retain control of Pharos. A second Roman fleet left Italy with a large army that was landed near Apollonia, where the first Illyrian force that had taken Corcyra met them. The united Roman forces then proceeded to Epidamnus, where they lifted the siege, and then carried on to the island of Issa, which they also freed.[25] Corcyra, Apollonia, Epidamnus and Issa all made friendship agreements with Rome,[26] although no formal commitments were made by any of the parties.

The Romans had sent a considerable force against the Illyrians, totalling some 200 warships manned by what were now veteran crews who had only recently finished fighting in the first Punic War which had ended in 241 BC. The Illyrians themselves probably had a very similar number of ships to the Romans, but it must be remembered that these were much lighter vessels not intended to be used in head-to-head combat against a fleet of larger vessels and in reality they stood very little chance against such a large and experienced Roman force. At first glance, the Roman fleet may even seem somewhat excessive. However, the Romans certainly bore in mind that the Illyrians were allies of the Macedonians, so it could well be that the size of the fleet was at least in part intended to dissuade the Macedonians from joining the fray. Additionally, unlike their opponents, it should also be remembered that these waters were unfamiliar to the Romans and their decision to send such a large fleet can in part be ascribed to their desire not to be caught by surprise.

The issues facing the Romans in the Adriatic were as much economic as they were strategic. Economically, Illyrian piracy threatened seaborne trade. Strategically, Illyrian control of the Adriatic and their alliance with the king of Macedon could have been very bad for Rome geopolitically. After having been thoroughly defeated by the Romans, Queen Teuta requested a peace treaty and an end to the war. The Romans agreed to grant her a treaty in 228 BC but in turn obliged the Illyrian forces to leave all those places that had been liberated by the Romans and furthermore they were not to sail past Lissus with more than two unarmed ships for any reason.[27] Teuta, left with little choice, accepted these terms. The treaty conditions make it clear that the conquest and annexation of the eastern Adriatic coastline was not a priority for the Roman state at this time, which is further highlighted by the fact that the Romans did not seek to directly maintain control in the region after they had defeated the Illyrian Queen with the help of the traitor Demetrius of Pharos.

The Second Illyrian War

Less than a decade later, whilst the Romans had been engaged in a serious war with the Gauls along the Po River for three years, the Illyrian traitor Demetrius had now succeeded Teuta and married Agron's first wife Triteuta.[28] Demetrius revived Illyrian piracy, even though this had been explicitly forbidden by the treaty with Rome.[29] He also re-established the Illyrian alliance with the Macedonians and fought with them in a victory against the Spartans in 222 BC.[30] Apparently, the Romans suspected he had convinced the Istrians to abandon their treaty with Rome and disrupt Roman supply shipping. The Atintani, an Illyrian tribe possibly of Thracian origin, also abandoned their treaties with Rome and joined Demetrius. In 220 BC Demetrius sailed past the Lissus river with a fleet of ninety warships accompanied by the Illyrian general Scerdilaidas. They sailed to the Peloponnese where they attacked Pylos.[31] The attack was a failure, however, and the Illyrian force then broke up into two groups, one comprising forty ships under the command of Scerdilaidas returning north and joining the Aetolians against the Achaean League, while Demetrius plundered the Cyclades, after which he returned to Illyria.[32] During the next winter Demetrius and his forces attacked a number of Illyrian towns that were allied to the Romans, directly provoking Roman intervention and starting the second Illyrian war.

In preparation for a possible Roman response to his actions, Demetrius stationed 6,000 of his best troops, which had been very well supplied, in the fortress on his home island of Pharos, and also garrisoned the fortress of Dimale which was located near Apollonia.[33] The Romans did respond and sent both consuls to deal with Demetrius. Aemilius Paullus, the principal Roman commander, quickly realizing the importance of the fortress at Dimale for Demetrius's control of the area, attacked it in the hopes of avoiding a prolonged siege. He took the fortress in less than seven days, giving the Romans control of the region.

The remainder of Demetrius's forces were on Pharos, where they were well fortified and prepared for the coming Roman assault. Paullus, being well aware of the situation, was again determined to avoid a prolonged siege, particularly as the Illyrian forces had prepared for such an eventuality. The Roman consul devised a very clever strategy to lure the Illyrian forces out of their fortress. This involved an attack on the port district of Pharos. Paullus secretly landed his main force on the island where the Illyrian garrison could not see them, and hid his troops in the woods. Once his main force was in position, a small group of elite soldiers was sent to set fire to the port buildings.

The strategy worked, the small-scale Roman attack on the port proving to be just the lure necessary to draw the Illyrian forces out from behind their walls, believing that they heavily outnumbered their opponents. The Illyrians sallied forth from the safety of their fortress, and once they had far enough away from their fortifications not to be able to get back when they saw the main Roman force, Paullus gave the order for it to emerge and position itself between the Illyrian soldiers and their fortress. This very clever strategy saw the second Illyrian war brought to a rapid end without the need for a prolonged siege that might have lasted months or possibly even longer.[34] Demetrius, seeing that he had fallen into a Roman trap and realizing that the Illyrian chances of success were very slim indeed, abandoned his own troops and fled to Macedonia, where he died later fighting in Macedonian service. The Romans reimposed all the same peace treaty conditions that they had after the conclusion of the first war. Pinnes, the son of Agron, was made King of Illyria, and required to pay tribute, and possibly war reparations, to the Romans.[35]

Philip V and the Bastarnae, 179–178 BC

Philip V of Macedon had come into conflict with the Romans because he was trying to expand his influence to the Adriatic coast and because he had entered into an alliance with Hannibal who, at the time, was campaigning in Italy. The Macedonians had been known for some time as well-trained and well-equipped soldiers. It is likely that the Macedonians didn't think too much of the Romans as a military force at this time, particularly after their defeats at Lake Trasimene and Cannae by the Carthaginians. Philip sought to align himself with Hannibal after these Roman defeats on the condition that Macedonian interests in Illyria were recognized. The Romans, having dealt with the Carthaginian threat, naturally turned their attention towards Philip, and after several engagements they thoroughly defeated his forces in 197 BC and forced him to come to terms, confining him to Macedon. Philip attempted to bypass this restriction by negotiating with the Bastarnae and using them to dispose of the troublesome Dardanians. The Bastarnae were a people of probably mixed Germanic and Celtic origin who lived north of the Danube and were apparently willing to travel to get involved in conflicts some distance from their homeland. By the third century AD the Bastarnae had become more assimilated with the nearby Sarmatian peoples than those of Germanic or Celtic origin. The Peucini, a branch of the Bastarnae situated north of the Danube delta, were heavily involved in the resistance against the Roman occupation of Moesia.

Philip apparently hoped that the Bastarnae could firstly eliminate the northern threat posed by the Dardanians and secondly it appears that Philip's plans for the Bastarnae may have included using them to attack the Italian Adriatic coast in order to ensure that the Romans were occupied with war on their own soil while he reclaimed territory lost due to the treaty he had with Rome, knowing that without this distraction any attempt to expand his territory would lead to a Roman military response. Although this is largely speculative, at least one ancient author suggests that this was Philip's planned use of the Bastarnae.

After much negotiation between Philip and the Thracians, the Macedonian monarch was able to arrange passage through Thrace for the Bastarnae. The Bastarnae crossed the Danube and made their way towards Macedon in order to meet with Philip. However, Philip's death occurred whilst the Bastarnae were still on the march, which led to a series of problems in Thrace when the Bastarnae apparently found themselves either unable to purchase supplies or unable to buy them at reasonable prices. A significant percentage of the Bastarnae had had enough of the difficulties involved in the journey by this point and returned home. The remainder, however, moved straight on to Dardania as per the agreement they had made with Philip. This led to a full-scale war between the Dardanians and the Bastarnae and their allies the Scordisci and some Thracians.[36] The Dardani were forced to take shelter in their fortifications and quickly contacted the Romans for assistance. The Dardani blamed their situation on Philip's successor Perseus, at least in part in an effort to encourage Roman intervention to halt Macedonian aggression in the region, which was a significant concern for the Romans. However, King Perseus convinced the Romans that he was not in fact involved, which ensured that they did not become involved in the conflict. The Dardani remained holed up in their strongholds until the allies of the Bastarnae decided to leave the area. Only then, some four years later, did they sally out from their strongholds to face the Bastarnae and drive them from Dardania.

The Third Macedonian War

Although not directly the focus of this book, the Third Macedonian War is important because Rome's victory here made their desire for increased influence and control in this region clear to all interested parties. As such, the Roman expansion in the region led to a number of issues with native people living nearby. Rome's interest in Macedonia was the result of the threat Perseus posed to Roman control of the Greek world.

This war was likely the result of a number of factors. Firstly the Romans had had issues with the Macedonians for some time: they had been known to become involved in wars against Rome as they had done by allying with Hannibal, something unlikely to be forgiven or forgotten by the Romans. Even after the Romans had defeated the Macedonians and had signed a treaty with Philip V which saw his territory significantly decreased, the Macedonians seemed intent on finding ways of regaining control of their former possessions. This included the events discussed above, such as Philip's invitation to the Bastarnae to attack Dardania. Combined with Philip's use of the Illyrian King Genthius, this likely led to the Roman decision to engage in a third Macedonian war. Philip's successor, his son Perseus, had been busy making treaties with Illyrians, Epirus and some of the nearby Thracian tribes, which contributed to Rome's nervousness about Macedon's desire to again try to regain influence in the region which could have threatened their control of Greece. Although significantly weaker than in the times of Philip II and Alexander the Great, Macedon was still renowned as one of the two main military powers in Europe, with a reputation for invincibility. The Third Macedonian War ended with Perseus's defeat at Pynda in 167 BC. This defeat and Perseus's flight from the battlefield effectively brought Macedon under Roman control.

The Thracians also played a significant role in this war, Perseus having incorporated about 3,000 of them into the Macedonian army. Livy described the Thracian warriors as being 'like wild beasts who had long been kept caged'.[37]

Thrace

> The Thracians are the biggest nation in the world, next to the Indians; were they under one ruler, or united, they would in my judgement be invincible and the strongest nation on earth.
>
> Hdt. V.3.

The Thracians were made up of many tribes dwelling in the Balkans between the Danube and the Aegean. They were renowned as a warlike people who valued military prowess above the crafts of the artisan.[38] The Thracians had demonstrated their capabilities on the battlefield as is demonstrated by the ongoing popularity of Thracian mercenaries. The Thracians were particularly well-known for their light cavalry and peltast light infantry. Thracian peltasts generally fought armed with javelins and were protected by a light wicker shield, often depicted in contemporary art as a hide-covered crescent shape known as a *pelte* or *pelta*, though shields of other shapes (circular and oval) are also known to have been used.[39] These troops often possessed a secondary weapon, the most common being the *sica*, a curved dagger, but clubs and swords were not unheard of either.[40] Peltasts performed the role of skirmishers, taking advantage of their mobility to run towards their enemy, hurl their javelins and then move out of harm's way. Peltasts were cheap troops to field as they didn't required the expensive equipment of their more heavily-armoured contemporaries, and their mobility made them very useful on a battlefield: they could be used to hold difficult terrain, ambush enemy forces or engage in costly hit-and-run tactics. Thracian peltasts were particularly well-regarded because of their ferocity in battle and the fact that they would engage in melee combat when necessary. Peltasts had repeatedly demonstrated their effectiveness, especially throughout the Peloponnesian wars when combined-arms tactics began to be employed by some of the Greeks.

Cavalry seems to have been the other great Thracian strength. Thrace had some excellent horse-rearing country, and horses certainly became an important part of Thracian identity as is illustrated by the cult of the Thracian rider god. There is evidence to suggest that Thracian horses were larger than the nearby steppe horses used by the Scythians. They were able to field a variety of cavalry types but seem to have favoured javelin-throwing light cavalry. Webber advances an interesting theory for why there isn't evidence of wider use of heavy cavalry: he suggests that the lack of centralization in Thrace ensured that the individual tribal groupings, although large enough to field cavalry forces, were generally not large enough to be able to afford significant numbers of heavy cavalry which would have been a lot more costly.[41]

According to Livy, even before the annexation of Macedonia in 146 BC the Thracians were considered by some Romans to be a greater threat to their control in the region than Macedonia itself was.

> The kings of Macedonia were thought to be dangerous to the liberty of Greece. Suppose that kingdom and nation extirpated, the Thracians, Illyrians, and in time the Gauls, (nations not subjugated and savage) would pour themselves into Macedonia first, and then into Greece. That they should not, by removing inconveniences which lay nearest, open a passage to others greater and more grievous.
>
> Livy, XXXIII.12.

Interestingly Livy is also clearly showing that the Romans believed that Macedonia functioned as a bulwark against a Thracian advance on Greece with hordes of warriors, which explains the lengths the Romans went to in order to hold Macedonia once they had taken it. Rome had a significant history in this region but interestingly there is no clearly-defined conquest rather a staged increase of influence that sees Rome gradually exert control in the region.

The Third Illyrian War

Some fifty years after the events of the second Illyrian war, another significant conflict erupted between Rome and the Illyrians. This third Illyrian war is more correctly described as part of the third Macedonian war than a separate conflict. The last Macedonian king, Perseus, bought the loyalty of the new Illyrian monarch, Genthius who had become King of Illyricum sometime before 180 BC. There is no evidence to suggest that the Illyrian king had been involved in any anti-Roman activities prior to his arrangement with Perseus, although there were allegations of renewed Illyrian piracy which Genthius strongly denied and as no action was taken against him it seems likely that the Romans believed that he was not directly involved.

Perseus convinced Genthius to support him during the third Macedonian war by promising to pay the Illyrian King a total of 300 talents, 10 of which was paid in advance.[42] Two Roman envoys were sent to the Illyrian king, who ordered that they be seized and held prisoner, accusing them of being spies rather than envoys. As a result Perseus cancelled the remaining payments to the Illyrians. Perseus seems to have thoughy that because Genthius had taken the Roman envoys hostage, he felt sure that even if he didn't pay the outstanding amount the Illyrians had made themselves an enemy of Rome. The Illyrians raised an army of about 15,000 men which they assembled at Lissus and then proceeded to attack the nearby Roman town of Bassania.[43] The Illyrians apparently also tried to use their fleet to disrupt the Roman supply ships in the region of Dyrrachium and Apollonia but they were defeated before being able to achieve any noteworthy damage.[44] Little is known about this war other than the fact that it ended, according to Appian, in less than twenty days, before news of its outbreak had even reached Rome,[45] with the surrender of Genthius after he had been trapped in his capital of Scodra, which was very well defended by the geography surrounding it and by the Illyrian army. Livy even suggests that the fortifications and manpower available were significant enough that had they manned their walls they might well have beaten the Roman forces off.[46] As it was, however, the Illyrian forces, rather than barricading themselves inside the fortress and fighting from the walls, left their fortifications to fight Romans in a flat area in front of the citadel. This worked very much in the Romans' favour, who easily beat the Illyrians, forcing their monarch to surrender. Genthius was sent to Rome, and five commissioners were desptached to Illyria to settle matters to the Senate's satisfaction. Again the Romans removed their garrisons from the region, demonstrating that they, as yet, had no intention to permanently annex it. Peoples who had allied themselves with Rome before the defeat of the Illyrian king were rewarded by an exemption from paying tribute. The Romans did not establish a province in Illyricum. The Roman praetor responsible for the Illyrian defeat, Anicius, celebrated a triumph in Rome early in 167 BC, the Illyrian King Genthius, his brother, his wife and some leading Illyrians being driven in front of his chariot.

The First Dalmatian War

After the fall of the Illyrian Kingdom, new political entities, like the Delmatae, Iapodes and Pannonii emerged in the region. The Delmetae, who had been subject to the Illyrians until the accession of Gentius, appear to have been the most formidable opponents the Romans faced in this region after the defeat of the Illyrians.[47] The Delmatian alliance that emerged was centred on city of Delmium, which was located on the coastal side of the Dinaric Mountains, facing the Adriatic. The alliance grew in part as a result of absorbing nearby small culturally-aligned communities. There is debate about the nature of the alliance and whether it actually had any effect in peacetime or whether it only came into effect in times of war.

The Delmatae quickly came to Rome's attention because of their increasing dominance in the region after the fall of the Illyrians. Perhaps the greatest strength of the Delmetae was their extensive hill fort (*gradina*) network. These forts provided strongpoints from which the defence of Dalmatia could be orchestrated. Many of these forts were located on promontories overlooking the plains, not on the mountain peaks themselves, not only ensuring that they overlooked important routes and important assets below but would also minimizing the cost and difficulty associated with their construction. They often relied on the naturally steep terrain on three sides instead of man-made defensive works for protection: where possible, walls were only used on the fourth side to protect the only viable access to the *gradina*. The walls were generally built of stone and topped with a wooden palisade. These well-defended positions certainly made the Roman assault on the Delmetae a hazardous and difficult undertaking.

The Romans moved against the Delmetae when the Greeks at Issa and the Daorsi, both Roman allies, called on Rome for assistance against them. The Romans sent envoys under the leadership of an ex-consul, C. Fannius Strabo, to the Delmatae in order to determine whether the complaints of their allies were justified.[48] When the envoys arrived in the region the Delmatae treated them very poorly, refusing them food and accommodation, not hearing their complaints and Polybius's account even suggests that they stole the envoys' horses.[49] However, this treatment certainly gave the Senate a publicly-acceptable reason for action against the Delmatae. Polybius suggests that the first Dalmatian war only occurred because the Senate and the Roman commanders wanted to keep their army trained and on an active war footing after a period of inaction.[50]

The first Roman commander sent against to the region was Caius Marcius Figulus in 156 BC who, having crossed into Delmetae territory from the region controlled by the Daorsi, was ambushed whilst setting up camp and forced to retreat to the Narenta River before trying to march his forces up the Trebizat valley to the Delmetae capital.[51] Again the Delmetae were ready for the Romans, who were able to achieve some relatively small-scale successes and captured a few minor *gradina* but in the end had to settle for establishing a blockade before the onset of winter. The following year the consul Publius Cornelius Scipio Nasica earned a triumph by defeating the Delmetae after a number of presumably hard-fought sieges of the Delmatae hill forts and culminating in the burning of their capital.

The Second Dalmatian War

The second Dalmatian war of 119–118 BC is described by at least one source, this time Appian, as a Roman commander's cynical and desperate attempt to achieve a triumph and the associated glory. Appian tells us that the Roman commander

Lucius Caecilius Metulus was greeted as a friend by the Delmatae and that he wintered with them at Salona, after which he went back to Rome claimed to have defeated them and received a triumph for his efforts.[52] It seems highly unlikely that any Roman commander could be awarded a triumph without any campaign having taken place, although there is no evidence that this campaign was as difficult as the first Dalmatian war had been. As a result of these campaigns the Roman commander was given the honorific 'Delmaticus', recognizing his efforts against this enemy. The region itself did not require Roman intervention again until after the Delmetae had taken control of Salona in 85 BC. It has been suggested that the Delmetae were possibly taking advantage of the situation in Rome because they thought the Romans were too busy fighting amongst themselves with the civil war between Marius and Sulla. However, a Roman force under the command of C. Cosconius was sent to take care of the interests of Rome's allies in 79 BC, again defeating the Delmatae after a two-year campaign resulting in the recapture of Salona but as before the Romans made no effort to permanently occupy any of the region.

Chapter 2

Julius Caesar

Julius Caesar also had problems in the region of Illyricum.[1] In 50 BC the Dalmatians and other Illyrians took the city of Promona, which was located close to the Adriatic coast, from the Liburni, another Illyrian tribe.[2] The Liburni appealed to Caesar for assistance, his response being to send a demand that the Dalmatians and other Illyrians who had taken Promona return the town to the Liburni. His efforts were fruitless, with the conquerors of Promona refusing to return it. Caesar sent a significant force to free Promona, but it was completely wiped out by the Illyrians.[3] Due to the outbreak of the civil war between Caesar and Pompey in 49 BC, Caesar was too busy to deal with the capture of Promona and the defeat of his forces by the Illyrians.

In 48 BC one of Caesar's generals, Gabinius, was trying to travel around the Adriatic from Italy to meet up with Caesar's forces,[4] but according to Appian the Dalmatians feared that if Caesar was victorious against Pompey that they would be punished for the defeat of the forces Caesar had sent against them not long before, so they attacked and defeated Gabinius's force of fifteen cohorts of infantry and 3,000 cavalry in a long steep gorge near Synodion.[5] This clearly demonstrates the Dalmatians's control of their home territory and how they could very significantly impact Roman forces trying to travel through the region.

The First Dacian Unification

Caesar had further problems in this region with a particular tribe based beyond the Danube, the Dacians.[6] The sources indicate that Caesar was planning military action against the Dacians immediately before his death, to punish the Dacian monarch Burebista for the fact that he had chosen to support Pompey in the civil war. As it turned out, Burebista's support had little effect as his forces arrived too late to participate in the actual conflict.[7] The Dacians are particularly interesting because they possessed a level of centralization and unification not seen amongst the other peoples north of the Rhine or the Danube, making them potentially the biggest threat to Rome in the region.

How the Dacians became unified during the reign of Burebista is far from certain. Little is known about pre-Burebistan Dacia, although what is accepted about Dacian society before Burebista's unification is that the tribes were already patriarchal, had strong social hierarchies and held warfare in high regard.[8] Like other tribal societies, the various Dacian tribes were engaged in incessant infighting prior to unification and it would seem likely that the only way Burebista could have convinced other Dacian kings to willingly submit to his authority was if he possessed overwhelming military force.[9] However, the fact that no war to establish his authority is directly mentioned in the sources might suggest that Burebista may have achieved unification, at least in part, through threat and negotiation rather than actual force. Based on Strabo's account of Burebista's accession, it is clear that the king of kings made use of religion to help establish his authority. He relied on the high-priest Deceneus who, Jordanes tells us, was given near-royal power.[10] After Burebista's death, Deceneus became a king in his own right, holding both religious and secular authority. However, the area he was able to exercise secular control over was nowhere near as extensive as that claimed by Burebista. There is some suggestion that after Burebista's unification, Dacia retained a level of religious unity, if not administrative unity. Burebista was able to establish control of a huge territory mostly, but not entirely, located north of the Danube which also included some Greek settlements along the Black Sea coast. During his unification campaign Burebista was required to defeat or absorb the many Celtic tribes that had taken up residence in Dacia.

The geographer Strabo tells us that a unified Dacia under the leadership of Burebista could field up to 200,000 warriors,[11] and that Burebista had become a threat to Rome because 'he would cross the Ister [the Danube] with impunity and plunder Thrace as far as Macedonia and the Illyrian country'.[12] The Dacian unification under Burebista differed in several important ways from the later one under Decebalus and as such both need to be examined and they demonstrate that the unification of the Dacians was what made them somewhat unique and a significant threat to Rome that needed to be dealt with.

Some have argued that Burebista's unification resulted only in an exceptionally large tribe rather than an organized state. It is likely that the truth of the situation lies somewhere between these two extremes. Much like his contemporary Julius Caesar, Burebista would have found himself in an extremely difficult political position by trying to impose a new form of organization. In both cases, they were trying to implement a system alien to their societies, although it could be argued that Burebista's differed less from the Dacian norm than Caesar's from the Roman one, as Burebista allowed the Dacian kings to retain their titles and authority whilst Caesar's ambitions have been suggested to be more extreme. In the end neither was particularly successful with their reforms as they were both assassinated by their peers in the same year.

During the reign of Burebista there is evidence of a distinction in social classes and a clear hierarchy illustrated by the differentiation between the *pilleati* and the *comati*[13] The *pilleati* or cap wearers, were the Dacian nobility and the *comati*, who are sometimes also referred to as the long-haired ones, represent the lower class of society. The vast majority of Dacian warriors would have come from amongst the *comati* but the warrior elite and leadership were drawn from the *pilleati*. Under Burebista's leadership Dacian society was still split along tribal lines for the purposes of administration as had been the case prior to unification, not based on territorial units like it was later, and controlled by compliant local kings.[14]

Construction of the immense Dacian fortress network in the Oraştie Mountains was begun in the reign of Burebista. This network became so large in the reigns of Burebista and later Decebalus that there is evidence for as many as ninety fortifications in the 200km² region which formed the Dacian heartlands. These fortresses were very well built by the standards of the day and would clearly have required the control of a significant labour force in order to have been constructed in any reasonable period of time.[15] Construction of these hill forts required significant alteration of the natural topography, including the digging away of the top of mountains, sometimes even down to the bedrock, and the building of terraced areas in order to create a flat surface large enough to accommodate the hill fort. Although the construction methods and significant features of the forts will be described later, it is important to note here that without a centralized authority to orchestrate their construction, they would have been nearly impossible to achieve because of the large amount of manpower required, the complexity of construction and the probable length of building time.[16] This sort of building programme also suggests that the Dacians had some degree of craft specialization in place. Craft specialization allows members of a community to specialize in something and trade those skills for money or subsistence goods. This concept of specialization is supported by evidence for a monetized economy.[17] Unlike many other tribal communities the Dacians made use of minted coinage. The circulation of local Dacian coinage suggests the existence of at least four independent Dacian principalities uin the second century BC.[18] The Dacian focus was on the nearby Roman civilization and we see a very large influx of Roman coinage entering Dacia in the decade following 75 BC. Apparently the Dacians couldn't get enough of it and there is significant evidence that they began minting imitation Roman *denarii*.[19]

The increase in the number of fortifications was directly related to Burebista's efforts at centralization, as is shown by the placement of these newly-constructed fortresses. The Dacian monarch placed forts in important strategic and economic positions often overlooking or near iron mines, salt reserves and commercial roads. These fortresses also formed a defensive enclave at the centre of which stood the Dacian capital of Sarmizegetusa Regia.

Burebista ruled for about sixteen years between 60–44BC. He mounted a campaign against the Celtic invaders that had settled in Dacia, expelling them from the region.[20] This alone demonstrates the growing strength and military capabilities of the Dacians under his rule. The Celtic presence had, however, brought some benefits to the Dacian people. They had contributed to the increased military capabilities of the Dacians and as a result to their own ejection from the region. One very significant example of Celtic influence is seen in Dacian ironworking capabilities, which improved dramatically as a result of contact with the highly-skilled Celtic craftsmen.

It was because of the Celtic ejection from the region, the Dacian unification, the very strong army held by Burebista and the fact that the Dacians seem willing to engage in Roman politics if they felt there was a potential for advantage to be had that the Romans appear to take the Dacian threat seriously for the very first time. At this point it seems likely that the Romans felt the Dacian threat was limited to the region of Illyricum, Thrace, the area of that would become Moesia, and the areas immediately north of the Danube: this clearly changes later.

Although frequently described as barbarians, the Dacian people were not 'barbarians' in the traditional sense, and the use of this term diminishes their achievements and sophistication. Under Burebista there is distinct evidence of a developing state organization.

This first period of centralization in Dacia ended with the death of Burebista. The Dacian king's death was apparently the result of a plot organized by other Dacian nobles who were unhappy about unification and Burebista's increasing power. Competition between various Dacian nobles after Burebista's death saw many of the centralizing features he had introduced temporarily disappear from Dacian society, which again split into a number of related but independent tribal communities. The geographer Strabo tells us the by the time of Crassus's expedition of 29–28 BC the Dacian people had split into five tribes.[21] This lack of centralization saw any threat posed by the Dacians reduced significantly, to a local threat like any other large tribal society. This is supported by the fact that the Dacians aggression, prior to the reign of Decebalus when Dacia was once again centralized under a single ruler, was limited to trans-Danubian raids, dealt with by various small to medium-scale punitive actions by Rome. The re-emergence of Dacian centralization under the Decebalus saw the Roman assessment of the Dacian threat and Rome's response change significantly: this is examined in a later chapter.

The turbulent early contact between the Romans and the peoples of the Danubian region which began in 230 BC when Rome's first trans-Adriatic expedition against Agron's Illyrians ended in 44 BC with the deaths of Caesar and Burebista in that same year. However, subsequent events demonstrate that matters between the Romans and the peoples of the Danube were clearly far from resolved by the end of this period. In the next two decades Rome was to undergo monumental changes including the end of the Roman Republic, the formation of the Second Triumvirate, a series of bloody civil wars and finally the creation of the Principate. The story of Rome's Danubian conquests resumes in the midst of these changes in 35 BC with Octavian's Illyrian command after a decade of Roman neglect and introspection, when matters in this region had again become volatile.

Chapter 3

Octavian's Illyricum

After Julius Caesar's assassination in 44 BC the Romans spent the next two decades in civil war, focusing their attention squarely on internal matters. A second triumvirate was established in 43 BC, this time consisting of Caesar's adopted son and heir Octavian, Caesar's compatriot Mark Antony and another of Caesar's commanders, Lepidus. After the triumvirs had dealt with Caesar's killers, they divided control of the Empire between them in the Treaty of Brundisium. This gave control of Hispania and Africa to Lepidus, Antony was given control in the East and Octavian took control of the West. Octavian, the most junior member of the Second Triumvirate, felt he needed a significant military success in order to be able to match Antony's reputation in the eyes of the soldiers and the wider populace.

Antony was a successful general in his own right and also Caesar's most capable subordinate, while the young Octavian's reputation in this regard was very limited. Octavian was, however, a very shrewd political operator and understood that in order to gain the reputation he desired whilst remaining in a position to affect what was happening in Rome, he needed to fight a campaign close to Italy. Antony was at this point campaigning in the East, trying to undo the damage that had been done by the Parthians, particularly in Syria and Judaea. These campaigns kept him well away from Rome for a significant proportion of this period and although defeating the Parthians would have been seen as a glorious success, his distance from Rome and Italy, combined with Octavian's very clever use of propaganda, significantly reduced the political value of Antony's victories. After conquering Sicily and deposing Lepidus who had had a falling-out with Octavian about it, the young triumvir chose to campaign in the province of Illyricum.

After a decade of internal struggles in Rome, a resurgence and growth of the tribes in Illyricum had occurred. Making matters worse was the fact that they apparently no longer feared Roman retaliation for aggression towards Roman allies and Italy itself. Several of these tribes had started raiding Istria, the Dalmatian coast and most importantly using the low passes of the Julian Alps to cross into and raid the north-eastern regions of Italy itself. This provided Octavian with a very good opportunity to portray his actions as measures needed to safeguard Italy.[1]

The conquest of Illyricum was begun by Octavian in 35 BC, this campaign representing the first concerted Roman effort to establish lasting control in the region. The level of success achieved by Octavian is still a matter of significant debate: in particular the extent of his conquest remains far from clear, with some authors suggesting that he conquered all of Illyricum and others suggesting only a small tract of Dalmatia and Pannonia were actually subjugated. In either event it cannot be doubted that there was some success. The main source for the campaigns of Octavian is Appian's account of the Illyrian wars, which is believed to be directly based on a memoir of the campaign composed by Octavian himself, which is unfortunately lost to us.

Illyricum was still not under Roman control when Octavian received it as part of his provincial command. As has been discussed in the previous chapter, Octavian's adopted father Caesar had history in this region, having lost a significant number of troops under the command of one of his subordinates here, but had been unable to do anything about it due to more pressing issues elsewhere. In the end Caesar's assassination prevented him from carrying out any plans he had for the region. Octavian's command here coincides with a crucial period in Roman history. The second five-year term of the triumvirate was due to expire in 33 BC, only two years away, ensuring that this period would be rife with attempts by the triumvirs to promote themselves in the run-up to the end of the triumvirate.

Octavian's motivation for choosing Illyricum is not completely clear. It is true that the tribes there had stopped paying the tribute owed to Rome and some had even started raiding north-eastern Italy but Appian provides us with yet another possible motivation. He tells us that Octavian wanted to directly connect Rome to the Danube by an overland route in preparation for a war against the Dacians.[2] As was mentioned in the previous chapter, this was in all likelihood Caesar's ultimate intention also. The region itself posed a clear threat to Roman forces in the area and any attempt to deal with the Dacians or anyone east of Illyricum was going to be hampered by the native tribes there. The failure of Gabinius's march through Illyrian territory in 48 BC clearly demonstrated the hazards faced by even relatively sizable Roman forces trying to move through Illyricum, ensuring that exterting any control beyond this region was extremely difficult.[3]

Conversely Dio, writing much later, ascribes far less noble motives to Octavian, suggesting that rather than being a genuine attempt at Danubian conquest and Roman expansion, Octavian's campaigns in the region were a result of his rivalry with Antony.[4] This rivalry meant that Octavian's actions in the region could provide him two tangible benefits; first, Octavian would be able to ensure that his soldiers were well drilled and ready for a war against Antony and his forces and secondly, as already mentioned, active conquest made him look a capable commander and the equal of Antony. However, in all matters of assigning motives to the great figures of the past, historians both contemporary and modern tend to try to explain very complex actions with a single simplistic motivation and it is just as likely that both Appian and Dio are correct. It is not implausible to imagine that Octavian's motivation for his Illyrian campaigns was both his desire to expand the frontiers of the Empire in an effort to prepare for an invasion of Dacia and at the same time demonstrate his military prowess in order to not appear inferior to his major rival. The political value of military success in Rome should never be underestimated.

Furthermore, there is evidence suggesting that the Iapydes, who lived near the Adriatic coast, had been raiding Aquileia and Tergeste which were important to Roman ambitions in the area.[5] Being situated very close to the Italian peninsula, any attacks against Aquileia could lead to concern about an invasion of Italy, contemporary belief in Rome seems to have been that Rome itself could be attacked as little as ten days after the loss of Aquileia. This belief would have contributed to the image Octavian was trying to cultivate with this conquest. Therefore, in 35 BC he crossed the Adriatic to deal with the Iapydes, Salassi, Taurisci and the Liburni.[6]

That the situation with Antony was on Octavian's mind throughout this period cannot be doubted. It is interesting to note that when some soldiers who had mutinied against Octavian and been discharged as a result wished to serve under him again, although he was very committed to discipline in the military forces, rather than refusing them, which might have resulted in them joining Antony, Octavian cautiously accepted them back into service. He did not allow them to mingle with the soldiers that had remained loyal to him and potentially weaken their resolve of these troops through their mutinous behaviour, but formed them into their own separate legion so that they couldn't corrupt anyone else. It is reasonable to assume that had Antony not been seen as a threat then Octavian would not have taken the mutineers back into his service.

Octavian's campaigns in Illyria lasted only two years, from 35 to 33 BC. At the head of ten legions, he marched from the north and subjugated the Iapydes, the Liburnians and the Delmatae.[7] Octavian led the campaign against the Iapydes himself, assigning the other tribes to subordinate commanders.[8] The Cisalpine Iapydes (on the Adriatic side of the mountain range) did not pose a significant problem to Octavian, but those on the other side (the Transalpine Iapydes) were much more difficult to defeat. Not much is known about the armies of the Illyrians and Dalmatians, leading many to assume that primitive military strategies and guerrilla warfare were the mainstays of Illyrian, Dalmatian and Pannonian warfare. However, a closer examination of Dalmatian and Illyrian warfare suggests that they were capable of fighting the Romans in pitched battles, conducting offensives, using captured Roman siege engines and even keeping the Romans at bay for extended periods of time due to the quality of their defensive works and the placement of their mountain strongholds which took advantage of the difficult terrain in the region.[9] Furthermore, in they also employed strong cavalry forces.[10] Although he would eventually conquer them, Octavian suffered a number of setbacks whilst facing the various fierce Illyrian tribes, including being wounded on more than one occasion.

Not much has been written about Illyrian warfare. Strabo tells us that the Iapydes were armoured like the Celts.[11] Long contact with the Celts in the region would certainly have led to some degree of similarity in their weapons and armour. The basic equipment used by a Celtic warrior would consist of a shield and a spear. Wealthy warriors could add a sword, helmet and mail armour. Celtic warriors, according to Strabo, carried two types of spears, a heavy thrusting spear and a lighter throwing javelin.[12] Helmets and mail were very rare on the Celtic battlefield because of their expense. What little is known from descriptions of the campaigns and Illyrian grave finds confirm that these forces were armed with a variety of weapons including spears, daggers, axes, swords and bows.[13] Some items that warrant specific mention include the long spears described in Appian's account of the Illyrian wars.[14] These were used by the Iapydes in their defence of Metulus to attack the Roman legionaries crossing the siege bridges from below. However, the most distinctive offensive weapon of the Illyrians seems to have been a single-edged curved sword, similar to the Greek *kopis*, known to the Romans as the *sica*.[15] This weapon is evident in the Illyrian archaeological record as far back as the Bronze Age and was also connected with the Thracians and the Dacians. The *sica* varied from between 40cm and 45cm long. Perhaps its most distinctive feature was that the blade curved forward like a sickle. The most famous contemporary artistic representation is on Trajan's Column where the Dacian king Decebalus is depicted committing suicide by cutting his own throat using a *sica*.[16] In exceptional circumstances the Illyrians were known to use captured siege engines, although they do not appear to have had the ability to manufacture or maintain torsion-powered weaponry themselves.

Defensive equipment has also been discovered in early grave finds, dating to about the seventh century BC, suggesting that the Illyrians utilized a small round wooden 'centre-grab' shield covered in leather with a bronze boss as their primary defence. The advantage of this type of shield is that it can also be used as an offensive weapon striking an opponent with the bronze boss, because the shield is not strapped to the forearm. Helmet finds seem fairly common in these early graves also. There are some very interesting and distinctive finds, in particular the type that has been called the Illyrian helmet and the unique Iapydes mail helmet which can be likened to a mediaeval mail coif.[17] Grave finds also included bronze breastplates and greaves although significantly fewer in number suggesting that, as elsewhere, they were the province of the wealthiest members of Iapydian society.

The First Campaign

The first campaign in the region in 35 BC started with Octavian landing his troops at the Liburnian port of Senia which was located on the coast south of Istria almost directly opposite Patavium.[18] Senia had for some time been the point at which goods from the coast passed on to the Iapydes, making it ideal as Octavian's base of operations for his Illyrian campaign as it was located close to one of the few roads that led through the imposing Velebit mountain range, providing access to the interior of Iapydian territory. Octavian's forces crossed the Velebits by way of the Vratnik Pass and fought the Iapydes on the Lika plain before moving southeast and accepting the surrender of both the Moentini and Avendeatae (the people of Monetium and Avendo).[19] Next Octavian made his way to the city of Arupium which was the most important *civitas* of the Cisalpine Iapydes. On his way there, the Arupini left their villages and took shelter in their city. However, when Octavian approached Arupium, the Arupini fled into the nearby forests without putting up a fight, allowing Octavian to easily capture the city. Octavian didn't destroy the city, however, but allowed the Arupini to return and continue to live there after they had surrendered to him.[20]

But the Transalpine Iapydes proved to be far more problematic to Octavian than their Cisalpine cousins had, as he discovered very quickly during his approach to Terponus. Terponus was the Transalpine Iapydian fortress located about 50km north of Arupium in the mountains at the end of an extremely rugged road. As Octavian's forces advanced, the Iapydes, like their Cisalpine cousins, fled from their villages and took to the forests. The inhabitants of Terponus further complicated the Roman advance along the rugged road by felling trees to block the road being used by the legionaries and ambushing the Roman forces from the surrounding forests, causing serious casualties when opportunities presented themselves.[21] Only Octavian's foresight prevented the Illyrian ambushes inflicting even more serious causalities on the Romans. Whenever the Romans were marching through a valley, Octavian made sure to station troops on the ridges overlooking the valley on both sides with orders to shadow the main force.[22] This tactic ensured that every time the Illyrians launched an ambush, the Roman supporting forces were able to counter-attack strongly and assault the rear of the Illyrian forces, killing a large number of them. When Octavian reached Terponus he found the city deserted, the inhabitants having fled into the forests. Again he chose not to destroy the city, hoping that he would be able to convince the people to surrender.[23]

The Iapydes of Terponus did surrender a short time later and, having come to terms with Octavian, were allowed to return to their homes.

The Siege of Metulus

The hardest-fought battle in this phase of Octavian's Illyrian wars was without doubt the siege of Metulus, located approximately 25km north of Terponus on a thickly wooded mountain. The town itself was built across two ridges with a narrow valley in between. Appian tells us that when the Romans arrived Metulus was defended by 3,000 well-armed warriors.[24] The Romans, rather optimistically, surrounded the city and attempted to storm it but were easily beaten off by the defenders. The Romans in response were forced to begin a formal siege and began building a siege mound. However, far from being cowed by the Roman technical expertise in siegecraft the Metulians repeatedly sallied forth day and night to make the Romans' job much harder and disrupt the building of the mound.[25] In addition, the Metulians used siege engines which they had captured from Decimus Brutus during the Civil War, while he had been retreating through Illyrian territory after the battle of Mutina in 40 BC.

The Metulians proved to be formidable foes, and the siege itself proved difficult for the Roman forces to bring to an end.[26] Dio suggests that the siege was so difficult that Octavian had to repeatedly send for reinforcements.[27] Although the Romans were having some success as their attacks were beginning to cause the walls of Metulus to crumble, the inhabitants of the city countered and began building another wall behind the original one, further frustrating the Roman legionaries' attempts to capture the city. When the first wall had collapsed under the Roman onslaught the defenders of Metulus retired to the second wall to continue the defence of their city. As a result of the damage inflicted on the first wall, the legionaries were able to capture it and they burnt it to the ground. To counter the new wall built by the Metulians the Romans were forced to raise two more siege mounds. From here they were able to send across four bridges which connected the two mounds to the top of the new wall the Metulians had built.

Octavian's plan for the capture of Metulus centred on these bridges. He sent a force to the rear of Metulus to launch a diversionary attack intended to draw off a significant proportion of the Metulian forces to the rear wall of their city.[28] Whilst the Metulians were engaged elsewhere, Octavian ordered his remaining troops to cross the siege bridges and capture the city. Octavian himself was nearby, watching how events were unfolding from a high tower. The assault did not turn out as Octavian had hoped, with some of the Metulians meeting the Romans on the bridges whilst the remainder of the defenders used long spears to attack the legionaries crossing the bridges from below.[29] Three of the four bridges were broken by the defenders and crashed to the ground, with a significant number of

Romans being killed or injured. This caused panic among the remaining Roman troops, who refused to cross the surviving bridge and attack.

Octavian came down from the tower from which he had been watching the battle and rebuked his men for their unwillingness to continue the assault, but it became clear to him quite quickly that his words were having no effect.[30] In an act of individual bravery, Octavian grabbed his shield, drew his sword and ran onto the bridge himself in the hope of encouraging his men to follow. Two of Octavian's generals, Hiero and the soon-to-be famous Agrippa, a bodyguard by the name of Lutus and one other Roman, Volas, ran onto the bridge with him. It was only when Octavian and his very few followers were almost all the way across that the legionaries felt shamed enough to follow him. Although exactly what Octavian had hoped for, the sheer number of men on the fourth and final bridge overburdened it so much that it also collapsed, with all those on the bridge falling in a heap on the ground below.[31] The collapse of the bridge resulted in deaths and many broken bones, Octavian himself suffering injuries to his right leg and both of his arms.[32]

In order to prevent a rout, Octavian quickly climbed to the top of his tower so that he could be seen by the legionaries and assure them that he was still alive. Almost immediately after the collapse of the final bridge, Octavian ordered the bridges rebuilt. This show of determination was what in the end convinced the Metulian leadership that they were unlikely to be rid of the Romans. The day after the battle of the bridges and Octavian's injury, the Metulians sent an envoy to the Romans in order to offer their surrender. The sources differ somewhat, with Appian telling us that the offer to surrender was genuine whereas Dio on the other hand suggests that it was all a ruse and that the inhabitants of Metulus had no intention of surrendering at all.[33] Either way, Octavian's conditions for the surrender were that he receive fifty hand-picked hostages and a promise from the Metulians to accept a Roman garrison, which was to be stationed on the higher of the two ridges the city was located on.

Unfortunately for all concerned, matters between the Romans and Metulus did not end there. The Metulians, a proud people, grew very angry when the Roman troops entered Metulus, preparing to establish their garrison and ordered the inhabitants to lay down their arms. They locked their wives and children in the council chambers, and placed guards at the doors with orders to set fire to the building if things did not go well for them.[34] The Romans, who were occupying the higher of the two ridge lines that made up the city, were attacked by the Metulians who desperately tried to eject or destroy the garrison troops. The Roman forces managed to overpower their attackers with little difficulty, killing the Metulian warriors to a man.

Seeing that victory was beyond their reach, the guards set over the Metulian women and children set fire to the council chambers. Appian tells us of women and children throwing themselves into the flames or committing suicide by other means.[35] The city itself burned to the ground, leaving no trace of what had been the greatest city in the region. The destruction of Metulus had a profound effect on the Iapydes, who were terrified by what had happened and almost immediately surrendered to Octavian, bringing the Transalpine Iapydes under the control of Rome for the first time. Having done what he had set out to do and in need of some time to recuperate from the injuries sustained during the siege of Metulus, Octavian returned to Rome, ending the first phase of his campaigns in the region. After he had left, the Poseni tribe rebelled. Octavian sent Marcus Helvius against them, the leaders of the revolt were killed and the rest of the tribe were sold as slaves.

The Second Campaign

Following his recuperation in Rome after the conquest of the Metulians, Octavian returned to the region. He then began a campaign against the Pannonians, which according to Dio was not a result of anything the Pannonians had done but rather because Octavian wanted to ensure that his troops received as much military experience as possible and he wanted to maintain his troops by forage and capture in enemy lands rather than by purchasing supplies himself.[36] However, the Pannonian campaign can also be seen as an important preparatory measure for a planned attack against Dacia. The area Octavian was campaigning in would provide him access to the Sava River which flowed into the Danube, providing a preferred route by which much-needed supplies could be transported to the front and Pannonian Segestica itself could serve as a forward base of operations in the event of a Dacian war.[37]

According to Dio, the Pannonians lived near Dalmatia along the banks of the Ister from Noricum to Moesia.[38] The same author describes the Pannonians as the bravest of all men even though they led, according to him, a miserable existence. Dio states that the Pannonian lands were poor and did not produce olives and only produced wine of the poorest quality, which led to the Pannonians drinking barley and millet-based beverages. He further describes them as high-spirited and bloodthirsty. Dio is exceptionally well qualified to explain the Pannonian situation to us as he was at one stage the Governor of Pannonia, albeit a significant amount of time after the events discussed here.

Octavian's campaign against the Pannonians began with an eight-day march through their territory in order to reach the fortress of Segestica. As with his previous campaign, Octavian's initial tactic was not to immediately devastate their villages, Appian suggesting he did this because he hoped to win them over.[39] Both of the major sources for this campaign make it clear that the Pannonians abandoned their villages and dispersed into the forests in order to fight the Romans in terrain less favourable to the legionaries. Octavian and his army advanced along the Sava River, with the Pannonians harassing them as they advanced towards Segestica, and it was only then, as it became obvious that he was not going to win the allegiance of the various Pannonian groups, that he ordered the destruction of their villages.

The siege of Segestica

Segestica was situated in an extremely important strategic location on the Sava river.[40] The Pannonian city was very well fortified, surrounded by a deep ditch. Octavian made it very clear that without Segestica any future action against the Dacians or their allies the Bastarnae, both located on the northern side of the Danube, was very unlikely to be successful. He tried to negotiate a peaceful resolution at Segestica in order to station a Roman garrison in the city so that it could be used as a logistical base for future operations on the other side of the Danube. His request for 100 hostages, food and the acceptance of a garrison were initially accepted by the city's nobility. However, the wider population of Segestica refused to accede to the Roman demands to station a garrison in the city, although Appian mentions that they had no problem with the request for hostages, knowing that they would come from amongst the children of the nobles.[41] At the approach of the garrison the people of Segestica shut the gates and manned the walls. This would probably have brought back memories of the events at Metulus for Octavian. As a result he was forced to besiege Segestica. He bridged the river and surrounded the city with a series of ditches and wooden palisades. The Pannonians made regular sorties against the Romans and their siege works. Other Pannonians tried to raise the siege of Segestica and render aid to their compatriots but they were repelled by a Roman ambush, ending the Segestani's hopes of outside assistance.

The siege lasted a full thirty days, although it has been suggested that this duration is not accurate and that the siege might have been significantly longer but was compressed by Appian, possibly in order to make Octavian look good. The city was captured by force but Octavian was impressed with the courage of the Segestani and as a result chose to be relatively lenient and only fined them. In order to maintain control of Segestica Octavian stationed approximately 12,000 troops as a garrison in a walled-off part of the city and returned to Rome.[42] There was a short-lived rebellion the following winter. When word reached him, Octavian led a rapid return to Pannonia to deal with the situation. The Segestani rebellion had caused the deaths of many Roman garrison troops, largely due to the surprise with which the Segestani attacked the Roman garrison, catching the legionaries off guard. The rebellion had been put down by what remained of the garrison by the time Octavian arrived. After having dealt with the Iapydes and the Pannonians, Octavian then shifted his focus south to the Delmatae.

The Third Campaign

In 34 BC, the Delmatae war-leader Verzo took Promona, located north of the coastal city of Salona, from the Liburnians in an effort to prevent Octavian's advance deeper into Dalmatian territory.[43] Verzo had assembled the majority of his 12,000 men at Promona, a well-defended fortress located in rough terrain surrounded by hills. He stationed troops on each of the surrounding hills looking down on Octavian's forces.[44] The Roman general secretly sent his best troops to ambush the Dalmatian troops on the highest of the hills. When they executed the plan and had killed the guards, they signalled their commander who then attacked the city. Octavian also made use of the captured hill, sending more Roman troops to its heights from where they attacked the remaining Dalmatians stationed on the other hills outside of Promona.

The Dalmatians managed to maintain their hold on two of the hills overlooking Promona, but Octavian isolated the fortress and the two hills occupied by his enemies by constructing a wall around them. After discovering that another Dalmatian leader, Testimus, was trying to relieve the fortress the Dalmatians in Promona sallied out against the Romans. Octavian's forces fought bravely and stormed Promona by pursuing the retreating Dalmatians into their city, whilst at the same time managing to prevent Testimus from bringing his forces to the assistance of Promona. Appian tells us that about one-third of the inhabitants of Promona and the Dalmatian leader Verzo were killed in the assault, the remainder shutting themselves up in the citadel for a final stand against the Romans.[45] After four nights the Dalmatians attacked the Roman cohort that had been set to guard them. The cohort was routed and fled in the face of the aggressive Dalmatian sortie. However, Octavian managed to force the remaining Dalmatians to surrender the following day. The cohort that had disgraced itself in the eyes of its commander was dealt with harshly. Octavian ordered the decimation of the unit: the men drew lots and every tenth man was killed, being clubbed to death by the other members of his unit. Additionally two centurions were executed and the survivors of the cohort were punished with reduced rations for the remainder of the campaigning season, as was traditional. It is particularly interesting to note that decimation as a punishment was very rarely used at this time and, other than a few rumoured cases later, Octavian may well have been the last commander to use it.

Testimus, thinking better of his plans, disbanded his army and ordered it to scatter, making it impossible for the Romans to hunt them down. Octavian then continued his campaign by destroying Synodion, which was located on the edge of the forest where Gabinius's forces had been attacked and defeated in 48 BC. Knowing that Gabinius's forces had been ambushed from the ridges either side of the long deep gorge, Octavian again flanked his own forces on both sides with detachments sent to the top of the ridge lines as he continued towards Setovia, burning any Dalmatian settlements on the way, including Andetrium which was located 20km inland of Salona.

Testimus and the bulk of the remaining Dalmatian forces had positioned themselves at Setovia. In order to defeat the Dalmatians, Octavian was again required to engage in a siege. During this siege another group of Dalmatians tried to relieve the city, but Octavian managed to repel them. In this fighting Octavian was again injured, this time receiving a knee wound when he was struck by a stone, putting him out of action for several days.[46] After this Octavian handed command over to Statilius Taurus whilst he returned to Rome to accept the consulship. Taurus blockaded the Dalmatian forces over the winter in order to prevent them being able to receive supplies from outside, leading to their surrender early in 33 BC. Octavian returned to the region at the very beginning of 33 BC to accept the Dalmatian surrender and the return of the Roman standards they had taken from Gabinius in 48 BC. Octavian received 700 children as hostages from the Dalmatians and a promise that the tribute owed from the time of Caesar would be repaid.

At the end of these campaigns Octavian was able to return to Rome and claim a triumph, and in a speech to the Senate named approximately thirty tribes that he had either forced to surrender or defeated. Importantly, he was able to bring Gabinius's lost standards back to Rome and to claim to have increased the prestige and safety of Italy and the Roman people, unlike his main competitor for political glory Antony, whose Parthian campaigns had not gone so well. In 33 BC Octavian's general Agrippa became *aedile* and spent vast sums of money on public works, including the building of a new aqueduct, and Octavian, cashing in on his military successes, became consul for the second time. Both used the wealth gained from their conquests in Illyria to promote their victories to the Roman people and advance their political careers. Additionally, Octavian had set the groundwork for a potential campaign against the Dacians: he now had access to the Sava River, which fed into the Danube, from Segestica if that was his intention. At this point matters in Rome occupied Octavian's attention for a while. It certainly seems likely that he intended action against the Dacians, firstly because it had been Caesar's publically-stated intention to do so and because they had caused trouble on the southern side of the Danube it is clear that some campaigns against the Dacians did take place during Augustus's reign as *princeps* and he advertised these successes in his *Res Gestae*. What is known of these campaigns, which is actually very little, will be discussed later in this chapter and the next.

The next three years saw Octavian at war with Antony. Through an ingenious use of propaganda, Octavian managed to convince the Senate to declare war on Cleopatra, the Egyptian queen and Antony's lover, thereby thinly veiling the reality that this was in fact another Roman civil war. With the assistance of his trusted and very talented general Marcus Agrippa, Octavian fought against Antony and Cleopatra, leading to a major naval victory at the battle of Actium in 31 BC which was closely followed by the suicides of both of his enemies in 30 BC.[47] With Lepidus neutralized and Antony dead, Octavian had established an unofficial principate and although he did not yet possess the full powers and authority that he soon would, he was essentially in control of the Empire from this point onwards.

Thrace, Moesia and the Southern Dacians

In 29 BC, the same year that the doors of the Temple of Janus were closed to symbolize the start of the *Pax Romana* (the Roman peace), the proconsul of Macedonia, Marcus Licinius Crassus, was called upon to defend the allied kingdom of Thrace from the invasion of the Bastarnae. Crassus had been consul in 30 BC and was made proconsul of the province of Macedonia in the following year. He was the grandson of Julius Caesar's contemporary, the immensely wealthy Marcus Licinius Crassus, who had defeated Spartacus, the Thracian gladiator who had rebelled against Rome in 71 BC, and then lined the Appian Way with 6,000 crucified rebels, and was later killed fighting the Parthians.[48]

The Bastarnae were a semi-nomadic people who first came to the attention of the Romans when they came to the assistance of Philip V of Macedon at his request in 184 BC. As described in the previous chapter, Philip's aims at the time seem to have been to mount an offensive against the Dardanians and possibly against the Romans as well.[49] The plan seems to have been for the Bastarnae to defeat the Dardanians, an Illyrian tribe, and remove them from their homeland in order to be able to settle there themselves, providing Philip with a trustworthy ally in the region and enhancing the security of Macedon.

The Bastarnae had a relatively close relationship with the nearby Sarmatian peoples as early as 62 BC when together they had defeated the armies of the Roman proconsul of Macedonia, Gaius Antonius, the uncle of Mark Antony. Dio erroneously describes the Bastarnae as related to the Scythians, probably as a result of the fact that they had significant interaction and assimilation with the neighbouring Sarmatian peoples by the time that Dio was writing some 200 years after the period under consideration here. Antonius, who was nicknamed '*Hybrida*' ('the Monster') because of his oppressive nature, was attempting to deal with Greek cities that had rebelled against the Roman rule in 62 BC when he was caught off guard by the Bastarnae who had crossed the Danube in 61 BC, apparently supported by the Dacians, to assist the Greek city of Histria against the Romans. Antonius's infantry were caught without cavalry support as he had sent them away, possibly chasing after a Sarmatian feint. The Bastarnae were able to surround the Roman forces and massacre them, leading to the capture of their standards. Some modern authors have suggested that it was the Sarmatians who had lured Antonius's cavalry away before the Bastarnae attacked and defeated his remaining forces, with the absence of their cavalry being a significant factor in the Roman defeat.

When Marcus Licinius Crassus was proconsul of Macedonia the Bastarnae again crossed the Danube and this time conquered the part of Moesia directly opposite where they lived. This open trans-Danubian aggression was not in and of itself significant enough provocation to bring the Bastarnae into conflict with Crassus, as the region they were attacking was not yet under Roman control and thus of little concern or interest to Crassus and certainly outside of his area of proconsular command. Had the Bastarnae restricted themselves to activity in the Dobrudja region, which was to become Moesia Inferior, they may not have come into conflict with Rome at this time. Crassus only took issue with the Bastarnae when they went further and crossed the Haemus Mountains (the Balkan Mountains) and started attacking parts of Thrace that belonged to the Dentheleti, who were allies of Rome. It was this that made Roman involvement inevitable: it is clear that Crassus wanted to support Sitas, the blind allied Thracian King, but perhaps more importantly still Crassus had to concern himself with the defence of Macedonia.

He launched a pre-emptive attack against the Bastarnae in Thrace which was designed to ward off a potential threat against his province. Therefore the threat posed by the Bastarnae not only to Roman allies and also to a Roman province was actually responsible for the Romans coming into conflict with the Bastarnae and subsequently the conquest of the region between Thrace and the area adjacent to the Danube in the Dobrudja. As proconsul of Macedonia, Crassus had four legions at his disposal, of which it appears that he used three in the campaigns against the Bastarnae, most likely IV *Scythica*, V *Macedonica* and possibly X *Fretensis* Crassus advanced on the Bastarnae while they were still in Thrace, the approach of his legions putting them to flight and they retreated into Moesia. Crassus and his legions followed. In the process Crassus took control of Segetica before being attacked by a contingent of Moesians, who had made the mistake of thinking that Crassus's advance guard was the whole of his army, and they were quickly defeated after Crassus brought the remainder of his army into battle. The Bastarnae meanwhile waited near the Cedrus River to determine the result of the encounter between the Moesians and the Romans. As the victor, Crassus was sent a message by the Bastarnae asking that he give up his pursuit of them as they had not attacked the Romans. Crassus stalled the envoys that had delivered the message, taking advantage of their love of wine by getting them drunk and quizzing them about the Bastarnaes's plans. That night Crassus moved his forces into the forests, his main force preceded by a small advance guard. Crassus had the advance guard take up position near the Bastarnae whilst keeping the remainder of his army hidden. The Bastarnae made the same mistake the Moesians had and attacked the advance guard, thinking it was on its own. The advance guard led the Bastarnae deeper into the forest where they were set upon by the remainder of the army. Crassus defeated the Bastarnae king in single combat.[50] The remainder of the Bastarnae split into groups, one hiding in a grove which the Romans didn't know about, while another seized a strong position and were besieged for several days before Crassus received the aid of Roles, one of the Dacian tribal kings, and defeated this group also. After that he turned his attention back to the Moesians, subduing the vast majority of them, but according to Dio not without a lot of hard fighting. With the onset of winter Crassus decided to return to Macedonia and put his forces into winter quarters.

En route to Macedonia, through the apparently friendly region of Thrace, the Roman forces were attacked by some Thracian tribes including the Maedi and the Serdi. Although there is no detail given about these engagements, Dio does tell us that the Romans suffered losses.[51] Meanwhile the Bastarnae, discovering that the Romans had left the region, decided to get revenge on the Thracian King Sitas and the Dentheleti who they felt were responsible for setting the Romans against them. Crassus was forced back into the field to deal with the Bastarnae yet again. He moved his legionaries very quickly into position by means of a series of forced marches. The speed with which the Romans moved caught the Bastarnae by complete surprise and they were quickly defeated.[52]

Crassus took this opportunity to deal with the Thracian tribes that had attacked his forces as they were marching back to Macedonia. These tribes were apparently preparing for war by fortifying their positions and were eager to engage the Romans. Again little is known about the campaign itself, other than that it was hard-fought and that the Romans emerged victorious. The Roman general conquered not only the Maedi and the Serdi but much of the rest of the country as well, with the exception of the territories belonging to the Odrysae. Captives belonging to the tribes that had attacked his forces were punished by having their hands cut off.[53]

Whilst dealing with matters in Thrace, the Dacian king Roles, who had assisted Crassus earlier, called upon the Romans to assist him in his war against another of the Dacian kings, Dapyx. Both of these tribes were located in the Dobrudja region that would become Moesia Inferior. Crassus went to the aid of Roles and was able to rout Dapyx's cavalry, forcing them to run into their own infantry forces thereby breaking them also. The Dacian army fled from the field, a great many being killed as they ran. Dapyx managed to retreat to a nearby fortress where the Romans besieged him. The siege was brought to an end, as many in the ancient world were, by someone inside the fort betraying their comrades and opening the gates to the enemy.[54] Dapyx and many other Dacians died when the fort fell, but Crassus did manage to capture Dapyx's brother who he allowed to go free unharmed. However, the fighting in the northern Dobrudja region bordering the Danube did not end with the defeat of Dapyx. Crassus pursued Dapyx's followers to a large cave called Ciris where many of them had taken shelter. Having located all the entrances to the cave, he blocked them up and starved the Dacians in the cave into submission.

Crassus did not end his Dacian campaigns but continued his offensive by attacking the Dacian King Zyraxes's strongest fortress, his capital of Genucla, which he had found out housed the standards taken from Gaius Antonius by the Bastarnae more than thirty years earlier.[55] In this assault the Roman general used a combined land and naval attack against this fortress which was situated on the banks of the Danube. Zyraxes, having heard of the imminent Roman approach, sought to negotiate an alliance with the nearby Scythians but was unable to return before his capital was lost to the Roman assault.[56] Crassus had actually defeated a significant number of Dacian tribes situated south of the Danube and it seems very likely that it was these victories Augustus refers to when talking about his Dacian conquests in the *Res Gestae*. It has also been suggested that Augustus deliberately played down Crassus's role in the Dacian defeats so that the honour of defeating the Dacians could be given to a member of the Imperial family.

In essence Crassus had managed to capture much of Thrace, Moesia and the Dobrudja near the Danube River north of the Haemus Mountains on the coast of the Black Sea. For his efforts Octavian awarded Crassus a triumph as a result of the defeat of the Bastarnae in particular, however he was not awarded the title imperator nor was he rewarded with the *spolia opima* even though he had killed King Deldo of the Bastarnae in single combat.[57] In terms of the Danube, significant inroads had been made and Rome had begun the process of annexation and occupation but the region remained far from pacified. The issue of Pannonia in particular was far from settled but Octavian's actions made the Roman intention to occupy and assume direct control in the region clear. The final conquest of Pannonia would again be delayed for approximately two decades and would be left to Octavian's most trusted generals after Octavian had succeeded in securing the principate for himself and taking the title Augustus.

Chapter 4

The Danube as the Northern Frontier

The region on the south bank of the Danube did not remain quiet for long. Although we only have the simplest of outlines for the events of the years 22–16 BC, they included several incursions against Rome's Thracian allies, Rome's first engagement with the Sarmatians and the ravaging of Macedonia by Illyrian tribes. These, combined with Augustus's personal experience on or near this frontier, are likely to have significantly contributed to his desire to move the northern frontier of the Roman Empire to the banks of the Danube.

We are informed by Dio that in 22 BC Marcus Primus, the Governor of Macedonia, attacked the Thracian Odrysians,[1] but unfortunately almost nothing is known about what occurred here or why, and this seems to be completely contrary to Rome's policy in the region which was based on supporting the Odrysians. Only three years later, in 19 BC, the Roman commander Marcus Lollius, who had been consul in 21 BC, was required to intervene against the Bessi on behalf of the allied Thracian Rhoemetalces, King of the Odrysians, in stark contrast to the actions of Primus. Lollius's intervention may well have been the catalyst that led to the transfer of the Roman army stationed in Macedonia to the new command incorporating both Thrace and Macedonia. In 16 BC Lucius Gallus engaged the Sarmatians in what was the first recorded instance of direct conflict between Rome and the Sarmatian people north of the Danube. The Sarmatians had crossed the river and were raiding the territory of Rhoemetalces. Lucius Gallus drove them back over the river in the same year.[2] The Dentheleti and the Scordisci, Illyrian tribes that were at least partially Thracian,[3] ravaged Macedonia in 16 BC. The Scordisci were dealt with by Tiberius in 14 BC, who brought them into an alliance with Rome that was to prove very helpful in the Pannonian war of 12 BC and later.

The Roman advance towards the Danube resumed under Augustus in 15 BC. The renamed Octavian was now the first Roman Emperor with direct control over the Empire's foreign policy. He chose to dispatch his stepson Drusus, the brother of the future Emperor Tiberius and father of the future Emperor Claudius, one of Rome's best generals, to deal with a new and emerging threat to the north of Italy.[4] Various tribes from Raetia, a region connected to the Italian peninsula by the Alps and sharing borders with Gaul, Germany and Noricum, had begun overrunning large tracts of Gallic territory, and to make matters even worse, some of these tribes, assisted by at least one Norican tribe, had begun raiding areas of northern Italy. This provided a clear reason and excuse for the new emperor to declare war against the Raeti and advance Augustus's desire for a northern frontier along the Danube.

Raetia

Raetia, located on the north side of the Alps, incorporated the area between the Alps and the Danube. Roughly synonymous with modern Switzerland, Raetia was bounded on the west by Germania superior and the Gallic Helvetii, on the east by Noricum and in the north by the Danube. Much of the region was very mountainous and not well-suited to agriculture. Not much is known about the Raetians other than that they were a tribal people most likely of Celtic origin. Although Livy argues that the Raeti were descended from the Etruscans, he admits any trace of Etruscan culture had disappeared due to the harshness of the environment they lived in.[5] Strabo clarifies, explaining that one side of the Alps was inhabited by the Raeti and Vennones and numerous smaller tribes.[6] These tribes were well known for their poverty and their willingness to make a living through robbery and brigandage.

Although the sources are relatively quiet about the Roman conquests in this region, Raetia was an important addition to the Empire and clearly illustrates Augustus's desire to move Rome's northern frontier to the Danube. Raetia's position adjacent to the upper Danube meant that if the Romans could take control of the region they would be very well positioned to dominate the Germans to the north and north-east, could take control of Noricum and gain direct access to the Danube which would have made logistics far easier for future campaigns against the Pannonians.

An enemy on Italian soil was a far from desirable situation for Augustus, who throughout his reign was at pains to maintain an image of peace, particularly in Italy which had seen too much military activity with recent civil wars. The Raetians were also making travel through or across the Alps unsafe for Roman traders or Rome's allies which would have caused Rome economic damage. The Raeti raids into Gaul and northern Italy provided Augustus with the perfect *casus belli*, ensuring that his actions appeared legitimate. To further his case for the legitimacy of this annexation, a particularly horrific story of the Raetian treatment of their captives was circulated and can be found in Dio, who describes how the Raetians executed all their male captives, apparently even going to the lengths of determining the gender of unborn children by means of augury and killing any who were thought to be male.[7] Stories like these were not uncommon when building a case for going to war, making it very difficult to determine the truthfulness of these claims, which at least in the eyes of contemporary Romans would justify Augustus sending Drusus and the legions against the Raeti.

Drusus's campaign started with a significant success when he encountered a force of Raetians near the Tridentine Alps and defeated them with little effort. As a result he was able to eject the Raeti from Italy, which would likely have gone a long way towards easing concerns in Rome about another barbarian invasion. Drusus was awarded a praetorship for his efforts.[8] However, the fact that the Raeti continued their raids in Gaul demonstrates that they were undeterred by the Roman success against them in the Alps. Consequently Tiberius, Augustus's other stepson, was sent by the emperor to deal with the Raeti in Gaul, pushing them out of Roman-controlled territory and back to their homeland. Tiberius and Drusus then combined in 15 BC to end Raeti brigandage and aggression in Roman territory once and for all.

In preparation for this combined assault, Publius Silius Nerva, the proconsul of Illyricum, was tasked with clearing and securing lines of advance into the Alps. The sources indicate that Nerva was successful in his mission, even though he had to leave the region prematurely in order to deal with a combined Pannonian-Norican assault on Histria.

Although, as so often happens when discussing the Danube, we lack specific details, it is clear that the defeat of the Raeti did require some hard fighting. The brothers, having forced the Raeti back to their own lands, invaded the region from multiple directions at the same time, hoping to prevent the Raeti from being able to assemble a unified force. Tiberius started his march in Gaul and Drusus started his in Cisalpine Gaul, making use of the routes cleared by Nerva the year before. Tiberius himself led an amphibious assault against the Raeti and Vindelici, crossing Lake Venetus and taking the enemy by surprise. In essence the two commanders carried out a very large-scale pincer movement, leading some forces themselves and using their lieutenants to lead the rest. Due to the speed and nature of the assault they were able to rapidly overwhelm their enemy, preventing them from mounting any form of unified resistance. The Raeti forces had to remain split in order to meet each of the Roman threats, thereby significantly weakening their overall defence. Split in this manner, they were essentially scattered across the entire province which made it easy for the Romans to overwhelm any barbarian force that they came into contact with. This war again involved the Romans fighting in treacherous mountainous terrain. Although the Roman forces faced significant dangers against an enemy that Velleius Paterculus describes as numerous and fiercely warlike, a combination of excellent commanders and solid strategy ensured that they suffered few actual losses.[9]

Tiberius and Drusus, by attacking from numerous directions, assaulted many Raeti fortresses and towns, as well as meeting Raeti forces in open combat and were able to demoralize the wider population and extend Roman control to the upper Danube. In the end, the defeat of the Raeti took no more than one summer of campaigning by the brothers. Although the victory, in the end, seems to have been a relatively simple matter, the seriousness with which the Romans approached this conquest is clearly illustrated by the fact that Drusus and Tiberius deployed as many as twelve legions in total for their combined attack, fielding in the vicinity of 60,000 troops.

After conquering the Raeti, Tiberius and Drusus deported most of the fittest men who were considered to be of military age. This harsh measure was carried out in the hopes of significantly reducing the risk of the Raetians being able to raise sufficient manpower to be able to launch an effective rebellion. It is also clear from the sources that enough men were left in the province for it to be able to function effectively and meet its tax obligations.[10] It should come as no surprise that from the outset Raetia was an Imperial province under the direct control of the emperor, as was the case with the vast majority of provinces that possessed a garrison. Raetia could not be left without a garrison at any time, not only to minimize the potential for rebellion but also because it shared a border with the Germans who were also considered a significant threat to Rome. However, there is no evidence of any concerted effort to Romanize the population or establish Roman-style administration in the province until the time of Claudius, several decades after the conquest had taken place.

Noricum

Noricum was located to the north-east of Italy and like Raetia was primarily made up of very mountainous terrain unsuited to agriculture.[11] Noricum was important to Rome for a number of reasons: just like Raetia Noricum was attached to Italy by the Alps, it bordered the Danube in the north and was an important supplier of raw materials, in particular high-quality iron. Norican iron was so renowned for its quality and use in the manufacture of Roman weapons that even the poet Horace makes mention of Norican swords.[12]

The conquest and annexation of Noricum is particularly interesting because from the least the first century BC most of the region was engaged in significant and mutually profitable trade with the Empire as well as many of the neighbouring Celtic peoples including the Pannonians.[13] Noricum was largely pro-Roman, as Strabo illustrated writing in the first century AD when he described Noricum in terms of three regions, with only the north-western kings seemingly anti-Roman.[14] The primary source of wealth for the other people of Noricum clearly rested on their iron mines, iron smelting and metalworking which the Norici were already renowned for during the reign of Augustus and which had probably begun as early as the fourth century BC. There is a significant amount of evidence that the trade was not only one way, with a great many goods originating from Rome or Italy found in the region, including glassware, oil and wine.[15] The quality of the one in the region certainly would have made Noricum an attractive annexation for the Romans as there was a high likelihood that province would be able to cover its own costs.

The Romans had encountered very little trouble from the Noricans, who seem to have been at peace with them throughout the period of Augustus's reign, with the exception of one tribe from the north-west of the region, the Ambisontes. It is the actions of this tribe that provided Augustus with an excuse for annexation: it seems very unlikely that Noricum posed any real threat to the Empire but annexing it was the only way in which Augustus could assume direct control up to the Danube. The sources indicate that at least the Ambisontes participated in Raeti raiding into Italy and there was also clear Norican participation with the Pannonians in the attack on Histria. Although these actions were not typical of the relationship between Rome and the majority of Noricans, it provided a clear *casus belli*.

There is very little evidence in the ancient sources for the conquest of Noricum: few even mention its occurrence and those that do often provide contradictory information. Therefore, there are a number of difficulties associated with our understanding of the conquest of Noricum, the first amongst which is one of the most fundamental questions: when exactly did it occur? Even the date of the actual annexation is disputed with suggestions ranging from 16, 15, 14 or 8 BC. Most modern authors now place it in 15 BC, with the Alpine campaigns of Tiberius and Drusus against the Raeti.[16] This annexation is largely overlooked by the ancient sources, making a precise determination of what actually happened and when very difficult. One ancient source, Appian, writing around the middle of the second century AD, actually admits that he was unable to find any details about the conquest of Noricum in his sources.[17]

The Romans were able to claim a *casus belli* as a result of the Ambisontes assisting the Raeti in a war against Rome, which is clear by a careful reading of Florus's *Bellum Noricum* (Norican War) which focuses mostly on Tiberius's and Drusus's war against the Raetians. Florus mentions the Norican Ambisontes as participants in the war and mentions that they too were defeated by Tiberius, but it is much more likely that the conquest of Noricum was the results of a change in Roman frontier policies, particularly in regards to the region north of Italy.[18] The fate of Norican was probably decided as soon as Augustus chose to send Tiberius and Drusus to deal with Raetia. He would not have seen any benefit in maintaining a friendly Norican kingdom next door rather than annexing it and making it part of the Empire. There were significant advantages to the annexation of Noricum and it is clear the control of this region would have helped the Romans establish control over the adjoining parts of the Danube which Augustus was planning to establish as the northern frontier of the Empire.

Appian is confused as to when the annexation of Noricum occurred and suggests that it was possibly in connection with Caesar's Gallic wars.[19] Dio, although not providing an exact date, suggests that Noricum was annexed as a direct result of a combined Norican and Pannonian attack on Histria on the Adriatic coast opposite Italy.[20] This attack, which occurred during the proconsulship of Publius Silius Nerva in 17 to 16 BC, does not provide an accurate reflection of the relationship between Noricum and Rome at the time. Nerva, who had been tasked with securing the lines of advance into the Alps for the planned invasion against the Raeti in the following year, had to suspend his operations in South Raetia where he had been fighting the Camuni and Venii, in order to deal with the Pannonians and the Norici. Dio's dating seems most likely, providing strong support for a date of 15 BC which would mean it coincided with the Raetian War waged by Tiberius and Drusus.

There is evidence to suggest that the annexation of the majority of Noricum actually occurred peacefully after the conclusion of the Alpine campaigns against the Raeti, the Vindelici and the Ambisontes, which goes a long way towards explaining the silence of the ancient sources about the Norican annexation.[21] This theory is further supported by the fact that although Noricum was incorporated into the Empire in 15 BC it is very difficult to determine what, if any, administrative organization was put in place by the Romans to control the newly-acquired province before the reign of Claudius and it appears that it was not made a province proper until then. This suggests that the Romans did not feel that their grip on Noricum was in any danger or that the possibility of armed rebellion existed, which is only likely if the bulk of Noricum joined the Empire peacefully. Before Claudius's administrative reforms, as there is no evidence of a Roman governor in Noricum, it seems probable that the governor of Pannonia assumed oversight of Noricum.

As a result of these conquests Augustus was able to open more roads and improve the existing ones through the Alps, making travel through the region much safer than it had been previously, the primary hazards now being the terrain and the weather rather than thieves and brigands.[22] Some thirty-three years after these conquests, Strabo wrote that after the conquest both regions quickly became peaceful and had remained so, dutifully paying their taxes down to the time in which he was writing.[23]

The annexation of Raetia and Noricum pushed the frontier of the Roman Empire to the banks of the Danube. The conquest of these two regions was strategically important for a number of reasons: it provided the Romans easy access to

A Thracian/Dacian *sica*. Not to scale. (*Author's photograph*)

A tanged Dacian *falx* blade. Not to scale. (*Author's photograph*)

A socketed Dacian *falx* blade. Not to scale. (*Author's photograph*)

Reproduction Dacian *falces* and *sica*. Not to scale. (*Author's photograph*)

Metope Number Unknown

Metope XVIII

Above left: Adamklissi Metope showing a Roman legionary wearing *lorica squamata* (scale armour) a *manica* and a cross-braced helmet. (*Author's photograph*)

Above right: Adamklissi Metope XVIII showing a Roman legionary wearing *lorica hamata* (mail armour) and a *manica*. The Dacian appears to be wearing a helmet and carries a *falx*. (*Author's photograph*)

Metope XX

Adamklissi Metope XX showing a Roman legionary wearing *Lorica Hamata* (mail armour) and a *manica*. The Dacian appears to be wearing a helmet and carries a *falx*. (*Author's photograph*)

Dacian warrior wearing looted Roman *lorica hamata* (mail armour) wielding a
falx. (Copyright Radu Oltean, *Art Historia*)

Sarmatian Horsemen riding into battle against the Romans, two of the horses are barded in scale armour as depicted on Trajan's Column. (*Copyright Radu Oltean, Art Historia*)

Roman Legionaries crossing the Danube on a makeshift pontoon bridge, on their way into Dacia. After the scene on Trajan's Column. (*Copyright Radu Oltean, Art Historia*)

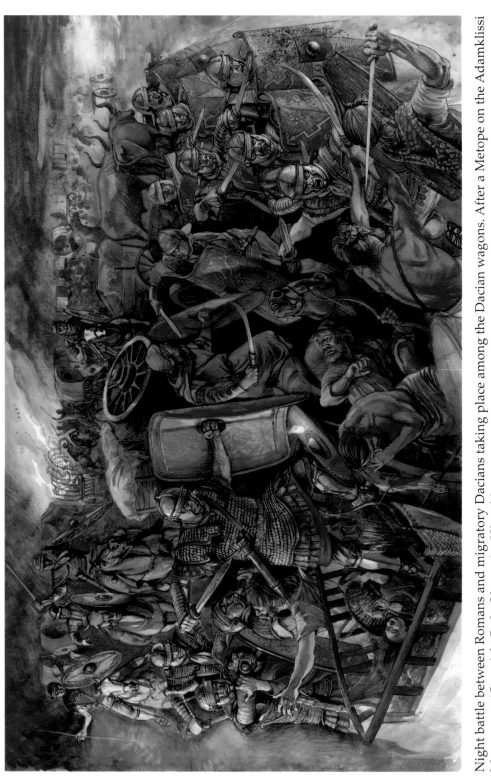

Night battle between Romans and migratory Dacians taking place among the Dacian wagons. After a Metope on the Adamklissi Monument. (*Copyright Radu Oltean, Art Historia*)

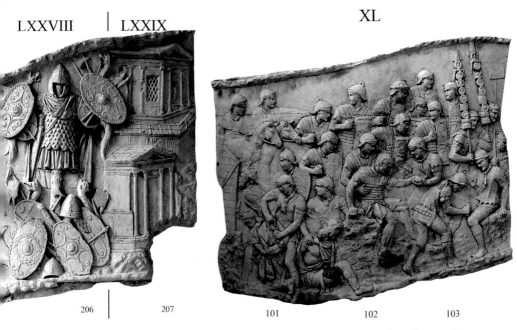

Above left: Trajan's Column Scenes LXXVIII-LXXIX. Victory trophy illustrating Dacian weapons and armour. (*Author's photograph*)

Above right: Trajan's Column Scene XL 'The battle of the bandages'. Injured Roman troops being treated after a battle with the Dacians. (*Author's photograph*)

Below: Trajan's Column Scene CXLV, The Dacian king Decebalus committing suicide rather than being captured by the Romans. (*Author's photograph*)

CXLV

Trajan's Column Scene LXVI Roman auxiliaries assaulting a Dacian fortress, two Dacians can be seen manning a Ballista on the fortress walls. (*Author's photograph*)

167   168   169

CXIII   CXIV

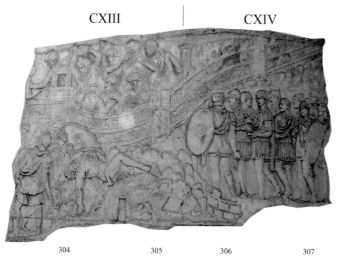

Trajan's Column Scenes CXIII-CXIV Roman forces arrayed outside the walls of a Dacian fortress, apparently made using *Murus Gallicus*. (*Author's photograph*)

304   305   306   307

Remains of one of the outer defensive walls at Sarmizegetusa Regia, the Dacian capital. (Gradistea Muncelului, Hunedoara Country). (*Author's photograph*)

the region between the Rhine and Danube, ensuring that the Romans possessed an additional attack route against the Germans, while it also provided a similar strategic advantage against the Pannonians to the east. Although the rivers may not have provided the defensive barrier that they were once believed to have been, they did limit the enemy to a few suitable crossing points and the Danube provided a clear delineation of the Roman and non-Roman worlds. Within three short years, the Roman army, again under the command of Tiberius, would seek to expand further east into Pannonia.

Tiberius's Pannonian War

Tiberius was an extremely experienced military commander by the time he became emperor in AD 14. At the age of 16 he had been fighting in Spain and ten years later he was sent to campaign in the Alps to assist his brother Drusus in putting an end to Raetian raids, which was the start of a series of campaigns on or near the Danube. Tiberius was the general directly responsible for a significant percentage of the conquests along the Danube, most undertaken during the principate of Augustus. Tiberius's own reign was marked by a lack of expansion and military operations on the frontiers, but under Augustus the Roman Empire underwent a period of significant expansion, much of which was focused on the northern frontiers the limits of which were marked by the Rhine and the Danube. The majority of the conquests in this region were undertaken by a handful of commanders personally loyal to Augustus. The generals involved in expanding the Danubian front included Marcus Agrippa, Drusus and Tiberius.

The importance of this frontier to Rome should not be underestimated, as these conquests significantly moved frontier disputes away from Italy and Rome. In part this was the cornerstone of the *Pax Romana* created by the Emperor Augustus and that much of his reputation for bringing peace to Rome rested on the conflicts and conquests undertaken on the Danube.

When examining the life of Tiberius, many modern authors focus almost exclusively on the period when he was emperor, and even neglect altogether or downplay his role as a successful general of Rome. It must be remembered that Tiberius did not become emperor until quite late in life, and although a rather dour character who undertook very little action on the frontiers whilst *princeps*, his youth was spent advancing the frontiers of the Empire and he was renowned as one of the best generals of his era.[24] It is also in this period of his life that Tiberius seems happiest, enjoying the company of the troops and life with the army. As a general he fought in some of the Rome's most important wars and demonstrated his abilities to choose the right course of action in any given situation. As is evident later in this chapter, Tiberius was able to formulate and follow successful strategies even against the emperor's wishes and even when the strategy in question was not likely to be the most popular one available to him. Although clearly he was not the only general to fight on this frontier during the reign of Augustus, Tiberius is undoubtedly the most prominent and important one.

Tiberius 12–9 BC

The Roman advance through the Balkans and to the Danube continued when Marcus Agrippa was sent to defeat the Pannonians. The Pannonian war that began in 12 BC demonstrates that Augustus, although having defeated various peoples in the region, had not established lasting control and matters here were far from completely settled during his campaigns in these provinces in the 30s BC. It seems that Augustus's conquests were largely limited the coastal regions, with very limited inland holdings such as Siscia. After returning from Syria, Agrippa, the most prominent Roman general of the time, was rewarded for his efforts in the East with another five years of tribunician power before he was sent to Pannonia. The choice of Agrippa is telling and clearly demonstrates how important the region was to Augustus and the level of his desire to see it conquered. Agrippa had earned his military reputation as Augustus's most trusted commander from the time of the civil wars against Antony, and was arguably the best general available to Rome at this time. Augustus was even grooming Agrippa as a possible successor to the principate, having arranged for his marriage to his own daughter Julia, which clearly demonstrated his position as next in line to the principate before his untimely death.[25]

Agrippa launched his Pannonian campaign almost immediately after being issued his orders, even though winter had already begun. It was very uncommon for Roman forces to be engaged in overseas conflict during the winter, even though ever since the Marian reforms the Roman army was no longer made up of farmers who needed to return to their fields. It was common practice that the soldiers would occupy a winter camp and not be engaged directly in a campaign during winter. This was for a number of reasons, most centring on supply and attrition.

Agrippa had been sent to deal with the Pannonians because as Dio puts it they seemed eager for war.[26] However, when the Pannonians realized Agrippa was on his way, their potential rebellion ended abruptly, demonstrating the power of his reputation as a general. However, unfortunately for Rome Agrippa fell ill and was taken to Campania, where he died by mid-March 12 BC.[27] After Agrippa's death, Augustus needed to find another general to take over in Pannonia, particularly because as soon as the Pannonians had learned of Agrippa's death they rapidly reignited their revolt. Augustus therefore chose the 29-year-old Tiberius.[28] The sources suggest that Tiberius was the only other general capable and competent enough to handle the very delicate and dangerous situation in the region. It is particularly interesting to note that many modern authors writing about Tiberius almost completely neglect this very important phase of his career. The Pannonian war was an extremely serious and potentially hazardous affair that needed to be quickly and effectively dealt with. To gain some perspective on how threatening the situation might have been to Rome, one need only look at the Pannonian rebellion of AD 6 when the sources indicate that they may have been able to be in a position to threaten Italy in as little as ten days.

Building on the achievements of his predecessors in the region, Marcus Agrippa and Marcus Vinicius, in 14–13 BC, Tiberius was tasked to complete the conquest of the interior. Unfortunately, although praising Tiberius's professionalism and skills as a general, Velleius Paterculus never delivered the promised full account of his Pannonian war which was either never written or is no longer available to us and what he does provide is significantly lacking in detail.[29] Dio's account is somewhat better but unfortunately details of this war are critically lacking in all of the primary sources and the modern scholarship alike.

Velleius Paterculus describes Tiberius's Pannonian war as a major and bloody conflict that was so close to Italy that it posed a major threat to Rome.[30] The levels of anxiety demonstrated at the time of the later Pannonian rebellion in AD 6 certainly gel with what Paterculus says and demonstrate the importance of Tiberius's war in this region and goes long way to explaining why two of the most highly-regarded generals in this period were sent to deal with rebellions in Pannonia and Dalmatia by Augustus.

Season One, 12 BC

In 12 BC Tiberius began his first campaign against the rebellious Pannonians. During this campaigning season he was able to overcome the Breuci located in the Sava Valley with the help of his allies the Scordisci. During his war in the region Tiberius received significant aid from this tribe, who had become allies of Rome. The Scordisci, an Illyrian Celtic tribe who lived on the south side of the Danube in the region near the confluence of the Danube and Sava Rivers, had been a problem for the Romans in the region for a long time, having been responsible for the death of the Roman governor of Macedonia in 119 BC and they were also the target of Roman military action in 110 BC when they were defeated by M. Minucius Rufus.

The Scordisci came into existence as a tribe sometime after 278 BC and were formed by some of the survivors of the Celtic raid into Greece, although by the time of Tiberius's Pannonian war it would be fair to say that they had become thoroughly Illyrian. In 16 BC the Scordisci, along with the Dentheleti, attacked Macedonia, but were working with the Romans against the Pannonians by 12 BC, so some time in the intervening four-year period the Scordisci were won over to the Roman side.

Where, when and how this occurred is largely a matter of conjecture. One suggestion that seems reasonable is that, immediately after his Alpine campaign against the Raeti, Tiberius subdued the Scordisci in 14 BC. Although this would suggest that Tiberius approached the Scordisci from the west, this makes sense considering the campaigns in Raetia and Noricum that Tiberius had been waging in the West prior to the alliance with the Scordisci.

Season Two, 11 BC

The second campaigning season in 11 BC saw the Dalmatians revolt, occupying Tiberius's attention, and whilst Tiberius was tied up with the Dalmatians the Pannonians, who had been suppressed in the previous year, rose up again, highlighting one of the critical issues throughout this period and in this region that led to situations where subdued tribes had to be dealt with more than once. This can be seen to stem from the way the Romans dealt with those that were causing problems. More often than not, when an enemy was deemed to have been defeated by the commander on the spot, the Romans moved on without instituting any control mechanisms either in terms of leaving a portion of their already-stretched military forces or setting up any civil organization to prevent a fresh outbreak.

Some of this must be attributed to the military reorganization undertaken by Augustus. After the end of the civil wars, he realized that the state could not afford to support the roughly sixty legions that had been raised for them, so he reduced the number of legions to thirty, thus halving available legionary manpower and as a result restricting Rome's ability to leave garrisons where they might have otherwise.[31] The Augustan reorganization of the military and the reduced force size made it more difficult for Tiberius to leave garrisons with each group he subdued, which inevitably meant that certain groups needed to be subdued more than once.

These repeated rebellions probably contributed to the official annexation of the region. Dalmatia was made an Imperial province as it was believed that not only did the behaviour of the inhabitants of the province require a garrison and this need was further influenced by the fact that the Pannonians were neighbours, and as had been demonstrated already rebellion there could easily spread into Dalmatia.

Season Three, 10 BC

During the third season of campaigning in Pannonia, the Dacians again drove themselves right back into Roman consciousness when they crossed the frozen Danube and attacked the Pannonians and Dalmatians, carrying off booty from both peoples.[32] It has been suggested that this Dacian incursion was the one that Lentulus responded to which mean that the date of this conflict be moved to 10 BC, but this seems unlikely. It is far more likely that this is a separate incident so, even though the Dacians had been pushed back from the Danube only four years earlier by Lentulus, they became a problem on the Danube again. However, this did not prevent further action on the Danube. Augustus, Florus, Tacitus and Strabo all mention operations on or beyond the Danube that occurred during this period.[33] Unfortunately, there is almost no detail regarding these operations or their date, although it is probable that Marcus Vinicius and Gnaeus Lentulus were the generals responsible.[34]

Interestingly, at this point it had been voted that the temple of Janus's doors be closed, signifying that there were no current wars. This was not a regular event in Rome, but occurred on a number of occasions during Augustus's reign, allowing him to claim that he brought peace to the Empire. On this occasion, the crossing of the Danube by the Dacians prevented the doors from actually being closed. The Pannonians and Dalmatians rebelled again, according to Dio because of the Roman imposition of tribute.[35] Tiberius, who was at the time in Gaul with Augustus, was sent to deal with them yet again and again Tiberius subdued them.

The Dacian Incursion of 10 BC

Whether it was his annoyance at not being able to close the doors to the temple of Janus or more likely in retribution for the Dacian crossing of the Danube in 10 BC, Augustus mounted a military campaign against the Dacians, apparently sending at least two generals into action. The Dacians, although nowhere near the threat that they had been when unified under Burebista, had demonstrated a continued willingness to become involved in areas that Rome deemed under her area of influence. Although it seems clear that this was not intended to be a war of conquest, the fact that it is mentioned in his memoirs demonstrates the importance of these campaigns and the spin that he hoped to apply to these events.[36]

Unfortunately, very little is known about these campaigns and no clear record of what took place is extant. What little is known is that Marcus Vinicius was sent to deal with the Dacians and the Bastarnae after the Dacian crossing of the Danube in 10 BC. What is recorded in the sources is that Vinicius managed to defeat an army of Dacians and Bastarnae and then forced the Celtic people living on the Great Hungarian Plain to ally with Rome. This suggests that Vinicius's focus was on the plains and lowland areas, whereas according to Florus another general, Cn. Cornelius Lentulus, who was also active against the Dacians in this period, seems to have concentrated on the highland Dacians.[37] Lentulus's forces apparently sailed up the Tisza and Maros rivers before entering the mountains to reach the Dacians. Although there is some debate as to when exactly Lentulus's campaigns north of the Danube occurred, it is a reasonable assumption that they were an element in the retaliatory actions against the Dacians for the crossing and attack of 10 BC.

Another argument for the date of Lentulus's campaigns is that if Tiberius did in fact defeat the Scordisci in 14 BC immediately after his Alpine campaigns, then it may also have been that year which saw Lentulus cross the Danube and attack the Dacians, although this is conjecture and far from certain. Perhaps the most significant issue with a date of 14 BC is that it precedes the Pannonian conflict, which begs the question what was Lentulus's role that led him to attack the Dacians. If he was stationed in Macedonia or Thrace that would make perfect sense as a defensive action against raiding Dacian forces, but it seems unlikely that Rome would push across the Danube while they had rebellious Pannonians at their back. Therefore, it seems more likely that Lentulus's campaign against the Dacians followed the defeat of the Pannonians or occurred immediately after their crossing of the Danube in 10 BC.

Based on the lack of detail about the campaign and its lack of long-term effect, it is likely that it was not particularly bloody and, as with Vinicius's campaigns, was not intended as a campaign of conquest. Augustus decided to attack the Dacians because of the trouble they had caused and their potential for continuing trouble along the Danubian frontier in a region far from comfortably under Roman control or domination at this early stage. The intent therefore seems to have been to punish the Dacians for crossing the Danube in 10 BC and demonstrate to them, their allies and other hostile 'barbarian' peoples that such incursions would not be tolerated by Rome. It is likely that a second purpose of these campaigns was to push the Dacians and others further away from the Danube itself, creating a more secure frontier along the river by partially clearing the northern bank of potentially hostile peoples.

Lentulus's and Vinicius's campaigns against the Dacians, Bastarnae and Sarmatians are the ones referred to by Augustus in the *Res Gestae* where he informs his readers that under his auspices Roman armies crossed the Danube and compelled the Dacian people to submit to the will of Rome, a clear exaggeration of actual events.[38] Clearly the actions of Augustus's generals against the Dacians did not prevent future aggression, with a renewal of attacks towards the end of Augustus's reign in AD 6, demonstrating that Augustus's comments in the *Res Gestae* were at best an optimistic assessment of the effect Vinicius's and Lentulus's campaigns had had. At this point the Dacians had not yet re-instituted any form of the unification they had achieved under the leadership of Burebista and would again under Decebalus. Strabo indicates that at this time Dacia was split between four or five different tribes controlled by their own kings, making them much less of an overall threat.[39] Like other tribal peoples that Rome had faced, it would have been difficult to put an end to the Dacian threat at this point because this would involve defeating all of the tribes simultaneously in order not to allow one defeated tribe to rebuild its strength while Roman forces were engaged against another, a situation seen in Germany.

Season Four, 9 BC

9 BC saw the continuation of Tiberius's Pannonian campaigns. The Pannonians and Dalmatians had once again rebelled against the authority of Rome. Having defeated them, Tiberius was at Ticinum, and it was here that he received word that his brother Drusus had been badly injured. Drusus was returning from his campaigns in Germany where he had advanced the Roman cause as far as the Elbe, when he took a serious fall from his horse. Tiberius, hearing the news, rushed to Drusus's side. He managed to see him before he died and accompanied his body back to Rome.[40]

Season Five, 8 BC

The final stage of the defeat of the Pannonians and Dalmatians was given over to Sextus Appuleius who took over from Tiberius in 8 BC and completed the conquest of the region, advancing the frontier of Illyricum to the Danube. The conquest was largely complete and Tiberius's skills were required elsewhere. He had been sent north to cross the Rhine and wage a campaign against the Germans, taking up where Drusus had left off when he died.

For his efforts in Illyricum Tiberius was granted an *ovatio* (the equestrian triumph), but he was not allowed to keep the title *imperator* bestowed on him by his troops

> Dalmatia, in rebellion for two hundred and twenty years, was pacified.
> Velleius Paterculus, II.90.1.

Velleius Paterculus believed this conquest of the Pannonians and Dalmatians ended the wars that had started in this region in 229 BC, from the first Illyrian war to the defeat of the Dalmatians and Pannonians by Tiberius some 220 years later.

The biggest advantage the Romans had from the period of the first Illyrian wars until the Pannonian rebellion of AD 6 was that the Pannonians and Dalmatians, unlike the Dacians, showed absolutely no tendency towards any form of unification or centralization. This made them far less of a threat militarily than the Dacians were to become under the control of a single leader.

The takeover of Noricum and the conquest of Pannonia together gave Rome control of the Drava and Sava valleys and hence the region encompassing the middle Danube. After the defeat of the Pannonians Tiberius had the men of military age disarmed and then sold as slaves. In 6 BC he decided to retire from public life, going into voluntary exile on Rhodes, which was to last about 10 years until 4 AD leaving Rome without its most competent and experienced general for a decade.[41]

Augustus's assessment of Tiberius's Pannonian Wars is clearly expressed in his *Res Gestae*:

> I subjected to Roman rule, through Tiberius Nero who was then my step-son and legate, certain Pannonian tribes that had not been reached by a Roman army before my reign, thereby extending the frontier of Illyricum as far as the Danube.

Despite Augustus's assertions the Danube was far from pacified, it is not even clear how much of the Danube had been reached, let alone how much territory was under Roman control. Even the Pannonians, who had borne the brunt of Tiberius's campaigns, did not remain pacified for much more than a decade.

Chapter 5

The Pannonian Uprising of AD 6 to 9

But when the revolt of Illyricum was reported he was transferred to the charge of a new war, the most serious of foreign wars since the Punic.

Suet., *Tib*. 16.

Tiberius remained in retirement on Rhodes until AD 4, returning to command Rome's armies in Germany.[1] The emperor's stepson was given three years of tribunician power to carry out this mission. Apparently matters in Germany were settled relatively quickly and Tiberius moved to Carnuntum in AD 6 in preparation for a war against the Marcomanni, who had settled in Bohemia north of the Danube River. It appears that they had moved out of Germany proper into Bohemia as a result of Drusus's campaigns, and as such it seems unlikely that they were in a position to pose any real threat to Rome at this time. However, the Marcomannic leader Marobodus was creating an autocratic regime rather than the traditional German leadership based on personal influence, which might have alerted the emperor to a potential future threat worth eliminating before it had the opportunity to develop into an actual one. Additionally, the conquest of Bohemia would have secured Roman control over central Europe. The plan appears to have been to trap the Marcomanni in a pincer movement between Tiberius's forces moving from the legionary base at Carnuntum and the forces of Sentius Saturninus attacking from the west.

The planned campaign against the Marcomanni was not in fact to happen because of the very serious revolt of the Pannonians and Dalmatians in AD 6.[2] This rebellion was described by Suetonius in his *Life of Tiberius* as the most serious foreign war since the war against Hannibal some two centuries earlier.[3] It has been suggested that this might be somewhat of an exaggeration but equally Suetonius's words should not be dismissed without due consideration. Suetonius tells us that Tiberius was given fifteen legions and a similar number of auxiliaries in order to put down this rebellion, approximately half of the Empire's available military might, which illustrates just how dangerous this rebellion was deemed to be by some in Rome.

A major consideration that would certainly have been taken into account when deciding the significance of the rebellion and the forces to be dispatched to deal with it was the proximity of Pannonia and Dalmatia to Rome and Italy.[4] This would certainly have contributed to the sense of dread felt in Rome. Add to this the fact that if the Pannonians and Dalmatians decided on a naval assault, only a short stretch of the Adriatic separated them from Italy, and as illustrated in an earlier chapter the region of Illyricum was full of accomplished sailors capable of orchestrating operations of this sort which had also been considered by the Macedonian King Philip V. Additionally, this region controlled the movement between West and East, making it not only important for the Romans to hold but making it difficult to bring their eastern and western forces together. The tribes of Illyricum had on a number of occasions demonstrated their ability to damage the Roman forces sent against them.[5]

Velleius Paterculus provides a particularly good source for this rebellion, as he was an officer on Tiberius's staff and actually took part in the campaign. Paterculus states that the rebels were preparing to launch an attack against Italy, illustrating if not the reality of the situation at least the greatest fear felt by the Romans.[6] Unfortunately, Paterculus never completed the full account of the conquest of the Dalmatians and Pannonians that he promised in his work which would have eliminated much of the conjecture about what occurred.[7]

The fact that both of these authors, one of whom was an active participant, suggest that the rebels were planning an attack against Italy clearly identifies how serious a threat this rebellion was believed to be by contemporary Romans.[8] Furthermore, Paterculus suggests that even Augustus felt that this rebellion could reach Rome in as little as ten days, an extremely short march.[9] Although it is true that Tiberius ended up sending a large proportion of his troops away, it can be argued that this was because of the nature of the strategy he chose or as a result of not being able to adequately supply an army of such size, rather than because he felt the numbers excessive to deal with the problem he faced.

The origins of the rebellion itself are particularly interesting as Rome can be blamed, at least in part, for giving the Pannonians and Dalmatians the idea that they might be able to mount a successful rebellion. Its origins can be traced back to Tiberius's preparations for an attack on the Marcomanni. Tiberius was assembling troops for this campaign when he called on the Pannonians and Dalmatians to provide auxiliary forces as they were obliged to do as provinces of Rome.[10] This was the first time since the conquest of 9/8 BC that the Romans had levied Pannonian and Dalmatian troops, and it seems that this formed a significant part of the reason for the rebellion of AD 6, as did the anger over the exaction of tribute by Rome's officials.

When the Pannonian and Dalmatian forces assembled for the first time in order to meet their obligations to Rome, they realized just how much military power was actually available to them if they acted in concert. Velleius Paterculus suggests that these forces numbered into the hundreds of thousands.[11] Additionally, the

Pannonians and Dalmatians would have been aware that a significant percentage of the Roman garrison in this region had been withdrawn to join Tiberius in preparation for his Marcomannic war, weakening and potentially delaying any Roman response to a rebellion.

Tiberius was at his headquarters at Carnuntum preparing for his campaign against the Marcomannic leader Marobodus with most of the Roman troops normally garrisoned in Illyricum when he received word of the rebellion. The prime movers behind it were two tribal leaders, both named Bato. The first was the chieftain of the Daesitiates who were based in the northern part of Dalmatia and the other the chieftain of the Breuci, the largest tribe in southern Pannonia. They were supported by a third chieftain, Pinnes, and many smaller tribes also joined in. The outbreak of the rebellion saw many Roman citizens who were in the region massacred by the rebels, as were any colonies of veterans which helped maintain Roman control in the region particularly when the legionary presence was reduced.[12]

In the first year of the rebellion, AD 6, the rebels orchestrated attacks against Salona and Sirmium and may have threatened Segestica which would have opened a direct route to Italy. Paterculus also suggests that they attacked Macedonia, clearly demonstrating that their ambitions were not restricted to freeing Illyricum from Roman occupation. The Roman reaction was for Tiberius to cleverly avoid contact with his enemy's main force. Paterculus tells us that the general's strategy was to attack only isolated forces that could be easily defeated.[13] This of course suggests that the rebellion itself was very dangerous to the Romans who were unprepared to face the unified forces of Pannonia and Dalmatia at this time. Tiberius's strategy was to prevent the spread of the rebellion as much as possible by restricting the movement of the rebels, temporarily surrendering areas that they had already taken control of and ensuring that Roman forces were concentrated on retaining strategically-important positions.

Paterculus makes it clear that the rebels were disciplined and well-trained, and it is also clear that they had intelligent and strong leadership at this time. The Breuci, under the leadership of their Bato, marched straight to the strategic garrison at Sirmium and would have managed to take it if not for the intervention of Caecina Severus, Legate of Moesia, who had the three Moesian legions, two legions from Asia Minor and the allied Thracian cavalry under his command. Sirmium was located on the Sava River and was important for the control of movement between East and West. There is some confusion about whether or not the rebels were actively engaged in besieging Sirmium and whether Severus lifted this siege or if he managed to engage the Breuci before they were able to reach the town. This confusion is largely due to the fact that Dio's account very clearly states that Severus defeated the Breuci at the Drava River, while some other authors suggest that Severus did actually lift the siege but then pursued the Breuci all the way to the Drava where he finally defeated them.[14] At this time, the Daesitiates had laid siege to the city of Salona on the Adriatic coast, but were repelled by the city's strong defences with their leader Bato being injured in the process.

As a result of their defeat at Salona, the Daesitiates retreated into the interior where they attempted to intercept the forces of Valerius Messalla. Tiberius, understanding the importance of Segestica, had sent Messalla, the Illyrian legate, ahead of the main force with one legion to secure this critical position. Although it is uncertain whether the rebels were directly threatening the town at this time, this fortress, which had been taken by Octavian in 33 BC, guarded the land route into Italy and its loss would certainly have intensified the fears of Augustus and the Senate dramatically. Messalla was able to take control of this strategically-important asset, so the situation in Pannonia at the end of AD 6 was that the Romans had control of the coastal cities and Segestica, but the rebels controlled the territory in between Segestica and the coast.

The Daesitiates moved east in an attempt to support the Breuci in another assault on Sirmium, which was prevented by Caecina Severus's allied Thracian cavalry commanded by their king Rhoemetalces.[15] Tiberius himself, with the remainder of the army, soon followed Messalla and occupied Segestica effectively ending any thoughts the rebels might have had of seizing this access route to Italy. Tiberius's quick and intelligent reaction to the Pannonian rebellion certainly minimized rebel successes in the first year but the Romans were unable to deny them all success. The rebels had very quickly seized control of a sizeable region of Illyricum, controlling most of the territory between the Sava River and the Adriatic but had failed to gain control of the strategically important towns of Salona, Sirmium or Segestica. However, to further compound Rome's problems, the Dacians again crossed the Danube in this year and began raiding Moesia with the assistance of nearby Sarmatian tribes, after Caecina Severus moved his forces into Pannonia to assist Tiberius. Tiberius ordered Severus to withdraw his forces from Pannonia and to return to his province to stop the Dacian-Sarmatian incursion as the opening of another front in the region could have been extremely problematic, particularly if others noted that the Dacians and Sarmatians were achieving success whilst the Roman forces were otherwise occupied. However, it appears that Severus's forces didn't leave Pannonia until sometime in the following year, AD 7. The Dacian incursion demonstrates that they were always ready to cross the Danube and raid Roman-controlled territory if they felt that the defences had in anyway lapsed or weakened. This pattern was repeated frequently until the eventual annexation of Dacia by the Emperor Trajan in AD 107.

Tiberius continued his strategy throughout the winter, as Paterculus illustrates by explaining the general's careful placement of Roman winter camps which were designed to prevent the rebels being able to access supplies and restricted their ability to move out of Tiberius's cordon and threaten the surrounding provinces, or worse Italy and Rome itself. The first year of the campaign for the Romans was largely characterized by manoeuvres designed to control strategic positions and inhibit the movement of the rebel forces rather than an attempt to engage in large scale battles.

AD 7

On their way back to Segestica through enemy-held territory. Severus's forces were ambushed by a combined force of the two Batos near the Volcaean marshes. Although outnumbered, Severus managed to win through to Segestica but his forces suffered significant losses in the process.[16] This battle might have been a strong contributing factor in Tiberius's decision to shift the Roman strategy from seeking pitched battles with the Pannonian and Dalmatian forces as Augustus seems to have wanted, to a strategy of containment. Severus and what remained of his forces were sent back to Moesia to deal with the Dacian and Sarmatian threat.

Tiberius's second campaigning season illustrates the strategic change employed by the Romans. Although apparently too passive for Augustus, Tiberius's strategy revolved around preventing the rebellious forces being able to access the supplies vital for maintaining their army. As has been demonstrated elsewhere, 'barbarian' armies largely relied on their ability to gather supplies from the land as they moved, not possessing the sophisticated logistical capabilities of the Romans. Tiberius's strategy cleverly utilized this weakness which had seen many German armies break up and return home before they had achieved any significant successes. Apparently, Tiberius's strategy rested on the hope that he could force the Pannonian and Dalmatian forces into a similar position.

Back in Rome there seems to have been a considerable degree of panic, Augustus seems had become very nervous about events in Illyricum and had ordered extraordinary levies and recalled veterans into service. In addition new taxes had been raised, and freedmen had been enrolled into the army.[17] In fact Dio tells us Augustus even went to the level of purchasing slaves from their owners, paying their value and the cost of their maintenance for six months, in order to be able to enlist them in the army to be sent to Tiberius.[18] These extraordinary actions had only rarely been taken before, demonstrating the seriousness with which Rome, the Emperor and the Senate viewed this rebellion. By doing this Augustus was able to send a large number of reinforcements under the command of Velleius Paterculus and further troops still under the command of Germanicus, the nephew of Tiberius, to Illyricum, whilst Augustus himself moved to Ariminum on the Adriatic coast in order to be better positioned to monitor events in Illyricum.[19]

Tiberius rapidly sent many of these additional forces back to Rome. To some degree this shows the difference in preferred strategy between Augustus and Tiberius. The Augustan strategy would likely have been a very aggressive counter-attack against the Pannonian and Dalmatian forces in an effort to end the rebellion as quickly as possible in a pitched battle or a series of them. Conversely Tiberius's strategy relied less on the number of troops that he could muster, and if Paterculus's numbers of Pannonian and Dalmatian troops are anywhere near accurate, combined with the fact that you have at least two armies involved, orchestrating a field engagement would have been extremely difficult and might leave the Romans open to a counter-attack by the second force. So Tiberius's strategy was to prevent the spread of conflict beyond the borders of Illyricum, and certainly keep the conflict out of Italy, and then to make conditions for these forces very difficult so that their leaders would be unable to keep them together thereby removing the threat posed by the Pannonian and Dalmatian armies.

Dio suggests that Augustus was concerned that Tiberius might be delaying the defeat of the Dalmatians and Pannonians so that he could remain under arms for a longer period of time and this is why he sent Germanicus to Illyricum with the hopes of ending the war quickly.[20] But the idea that Augustus did not trust Tiberius seems very unlikely. Augustus had the authority to send any general he chose to deal with the Pannonian threat and he chose Tiberius: he also had the authority to replace him at any time and chose not to do so. It seems more likely that there was perhaps some disagreement about the most effective and expedient way to win this war but it seems very unlikely that Tiberius's loyalty was ever seriously questioned.

For Tiberius the additional forces sent by Augustus would, rather than be considered a helpful resource, have been an additional burden, increasing his logistic problems. Considering his strategy this was probably the last thing he needed or wanted as a strategy of containment doesn't need as many troops as an aggressive assault and the fact that he was destroying supplies in order to prevent the rebels from laying hands on them meant that logically he did not want to increase his own needs. The nature of the forces sent to Tiberius would have further disinclined him from keeping these troops.

Tiberius's decision to proceed with the use of a scorched-earth policy in order to force the collapse of the rebellion, contrary to Augustus's desires, is evident. In this instance Tiberius burnt or otherwise destroyed anything he felt could aid the Pannonian cause. Although Augustus did not appear to have been pleased by this strategy the results became clear in AD 8 when the Breuci and their Bato surrendered, largely due to the hardship inflicted by Tiberius's strategy.[21] Dio tells us that the Dalmatians and Pannonians suffered badly from the lack of supplies and were afflicted by famine and then by disease because they were reduced to using roots and unfamiliar herbs for food.[22]

Bato, the chief of the Breuci, after surrendering to Rome, betrayed Pinnes and joined the Romans, receiving as a reward confirmation of his right to rule the Breuci. The Breucian Bato was then captured by the other Bato and put to death.[23] As a result many of the Pannonians rose up to continue the revolt against Rome, Silvanus, however, made war against them and defeated the Breuci once and for all. With this defeat the Dalmatian Bato saw that there was very little chance of maintaining the rebellion in Pannonia and retreated to Dalmatia where he occupied the passes with garrisons. The Pannonians, due to the activities of Silvanus, surrendered.

AD 9

Among other places, Germanicus captured Splonum in Dalmatia, which was described as being well fortified by nature, walls and a vast number of defenders. This defeat was not due to the use of siege engines or assaults but rather a bizarre incident that saw a German cavalrymen hurl a stone which shook up a section of parapet so violently that it fell, taking with it the man who was leaning against it. This so frightened the other defenders on this part of the wall that they abandoned it and ran into the citadel, where a short time later they surrendered.[24]

It seems that the war caused a famine in Rome and Tiberius was once again sent to the front. Furthermore he was well aware that keeping such a large army together for any period of time could lead to a mutiny that would itself threaten Rome as grievously as the Pannonia rebellion itself. In order to minimize the chances of rebellion Tiberius split the army in Illyricum into three separate forces, one under the command of Silvanus, the second under Marcus Lepidus and the third under his personal control, accompanied by Germanicus. This force marched against Bato. Dio tells us that Lepidus and Silvanus defeated their assigned opponents easily.[25] On the other hand, Tiberius had far more trouble defeating Bato, Tiberius and Germanicus spent a significant amount of time chasing the rebel leader from place to place practically over the whole country. When they did finally catch up with Bato, he had secured himself in the fortress of Andetrium which Augustus had captured in 34 to 33 BC. It was a particularly imposing structure as it was built in the mountains, extremely difficult to access, very well fortified and surrounded by deep ravines. Additionally, Bato secured his position by ensuring that he had adequate provisions in the fortress to withstand the inevitable siege and to make matters worse for Tiberius, the rebel leader had managed to ambush several Roman supply convoys, turning the tables on his opponents and putting them under significant logistical pressure.

The Roman forces clearly outnumbered the Dalmatians holed up in the fortress but the terrain was clearly in the Dalmatians's favour. Tiberius, realizing the nature of the situation, was unwilling to commit his forces to an assault against the fortress because of the difficulties of unified action in this terrain. However, the siege itself was proving pointless as the Dalmatians were too well supplied and any thoughts of retreat had to be abandoned as this would be seen as disgraceful.

The Roman soldiers, apparently disturbed by the circumstances they found themselves in, created a significant clamour. The rebels, camped just outside the fortress, perhaps thinking that the noise signified the onset of an assault, retreated into the fortress itself. In the meantime Tiberius managed to quieten his troops and maintain the siege against Andetrium long enough to make Bato believe that he could not defeat the Romans. Bato sent an emissary to Tiberius to discuss terms for surrender, knowing that the forces available to him were no match for the Romans camped outside the fortress. However, he was unable to convince the rest of the Dalmatians to follow suit. Accordingly Tiberius, feeling that the Dalmatians's spirit had been broken, decided to assault the stronghold without further concern for the difficulties engendered by the terrain.

Tiberius held back a proportion of his force as a reserve, to be used in case the main force encountered difficulties. He himself watched the engagement from a raised platform. His main force, formed into a tightly-packed square, advanced upon the fortress, but the uneven nature of the terrain soon broke up the formation. The Dalmatians formed up outside of the wall of their fort, from where they did everything they could to make the Romans' assault more difficult. They threw large quantities of rocks and stones down the steep incline at the attackers, and rolled wagons filled with rocks down the slope. Dio describes these rocks and stones as hitting with a force equivalent to ones shot from slings.[26] The tactic worked in that the Roman forces were separated even more than they had been by the terrain, and the Dalmatians capitalized on the Roman difficulties by throwing spears and shooting missiles at the advancing Roman troops. Tiberius's soldiers on several occasions almost turned and retreated, but the general, through the use of judicious reinforcements, was able to maintain their forward momentum. Simultaneously Tiberius sent a detachment of troops from the reserve in a wide flanking manoeuvre, catching the enemy off guard. Dio tells us that the enemy were not even able to retreat into their fortress but instead scattered into the surrounding countryside having discarded their armour in favour of speed.[27] The Romans pursued their fleeing enemy, hoping to inflict as many casualties as possible on the enemy forces in order to prevent them forming up again and continuing the rebellion.[28] After they had hunted down their fleeing enemy the Romans returned and took possession of the fortress as the inhabitants had surrendered.

Germanicus continued dealing with the remaining rebels, many of whom were being spurred on by deserters from the Roman army who knew that they would not be well received even if they surrendered. It was very common for a small percentage of Roman soldiers to desert and fight with the enemy: examples of this can be found in most major campaigns and often peace terms included a clause about surrendering Roman deserters.[29] Germanicus's army was forced to besiege the fortress of Arduba which because of its very strong fortifications on the River with swift currents that flowed around the most of the base of the fortress he was unable to defeat on his own even though he had a significantly larger force available to him than the defenders had. Apparently a great many Roman deserters were involved in the defence of this fortress, which led to an argument because most of the native defenders wanted to surrender and the deserters did not. It is particularly interesting to note that the native women sided with the Roman deserters in not wanting to surrender for fear of what would become of them and their children. The two sides fought it out inside the fortress and in the end the natives won, so that many of the women either threw themselves into fires or killed themselves by throwing themselves into the river below whilst clutching their children. After this, many of the remaining pockets of resistance in the nearby region surrendered themselves to Germanicus, effectively ending the rebellion. In the meantime, whilst Germanicus was dealing with the last of the resistance, Tiberius was organizing matters in relation to those who had already surrendered. Soon after Germanicus's victories Bato sent envoys, including his son Sceus, to Tiberius offering to surrender himself and all his followers if he was granted a pardon. Tiberius granted him an audience where in response to Tiberius's questioning the reasons for the rebellion Bato's supposed response is recorded by Dio:

> You Romans are to blame for this, for you send as guardians of your flocks, not dogs or shepherds, but wolves.
>
> Dio LVI.16.3

Although militarily a clear victory for Rome, the Pannonian rebellion saw a great many Roman traders, civilians and soldiers killed, enormous sums of money drained from the Roman coffers to pay for this war and in the end very little booty was collected. However, the Pannonian rebellion was defeated. Tiberius split Illyricum into the provinces of Pannonia and Dalmatia, neither of which caused serious problems again.

Chapter 6

The Dacians: an Emerging Empire

The Thracians are the biggest nation in the world, next to the Indians;
were they under one ruler, or united, they would in my judgement be
invincible and the strongest nation on earth.

Herodotus, V.3.

The Dacians played a major role in the events on the Danube for almost
half a century and over the reigns of six emperors. As such they warrant a more detailed examination in an effort to understand the nature
of these people that makes them such a significant factor during this period.
The emergence of Dacian unity on the western banks of the Danube must have
brought Herodotus's fears to the forefront of Roman minds, witnessing a people that had demonstrated clear hostility to Roman interests in the region since
at least the time of Caesar becoming a unified entity. The Romans understood
that the Dacians were related to the Thracians, the geographer Strabo indicating
that the Greeks too understood that the Dacians were a Thracian people.[1] The
only mitigating factor that may have eased growing concerns among the Romans,
probably came from the knowledge that the Thracian tribes displayed little incli-
nation towards unity.

The first evidence of unification north of the Danube was under the self-
stylised King of Kings Burebista sometime around 60 BC. Prior to Burebista's
unification, discussed in an earlier chapter, the Dacian tribes were disparate and
lacking any form of unity, very much like the other tribal societies in the region.
The tribal nature of the Dacian people certainly contributes to the confusion
regarding their identity. There are still ongoing debates about whether the people
the Greeks called the Getae are in fact the same people that the Romans called the
Dacians, some authors arguing that these two are in fact one and the same and
that the naming differences are due the differing practice between the Greek and
the Roman authors, while others, Oltean amongst them, argue that some Roman
authors refer to the Getae and the Dacians as separate people and propose that a
division should be made based on geography, so that those living on the southern
slope of the Carpathians and on the right bank of the Danube should be referred to
as the Getae and those living in the circle of the Carpathians and the north should

be called Dacians.[2] Realistically many of these arguments are based purely on semantics: individual Dacian tribes prior to unification[3] did not necessarily consider themselves as part of a greater Dacian whole and evidence clearly indicates that culturally and linguistically the Dacians and Getae were the same, and differed from the Thracians around them only in customs and religion. Therefore, in this book the term 'Dacians' has been used to describe both the Getae and Dacians on the assumption that the few Roman authors who did use the term Getae did so based on the influence of Greek authors and texts.

The Second Dacian Unification

After the death of Burebista the threat posed by Dacia significantly declined as its unity came to an end. For much of the period between the death of Dacia's first king and the emergence of its second, Decebalus, Dacia was seemingly a secondary concern for Rome. Only relatively minor engagements occurred and no concerted effort to conquer or annex the region can be found in the evidence. Decebalus, the second leader to unify the various Dacian tribes, became king sometime about AD 87. After the death of Burebista the Dacians had reverted to their former tribal organization, splitting into approximately four tribes, with some unification possibly surviving in the Orăştie mountains under the leadership of Burebista's one-time priest Decaeneus.[4] It is the period of Decebalus's reign, approximately 87–107 AD, that caused the most difficulty for the Romans and resulted in the annexation of Dacia as a Roman province.

Under Decebalus, unification took a slightly different and somewhat more sophisticated form than under his predecessor. In this system, chosen officials, drawn from the *pilleati*, were placed in charge of arable lands and forts with oversight of economically-important regions,[5] or important thoroughfares in order to maintain control of these vital assets and protect them from any threats. It seems that Decebalus's Dacia was better organized and more thoroughly centralized than that of Burebista. It is apparent that under Decebalus's leadership a distinction between the warrior elite, the *pilleati*, and the administrative and economic elite, the *tarabostes*, was created.[6] It is also during Decebalus's reign that emphasis was shifted from traditional tribal groupings to territorial regions which functioned as administrative units.

Dacian unification again became an issue at the forefront of Roman activity in the region. One of the primary reasons the Dacians came to pose such a significant problem to the Romans was the fact that they were able to achieve an uncommon level of centralization. It is clear that Rome was most concerned about the Dacians when they were exhibiting significant elements of centralization, as was the case first under Burebista and then again under Decebalus.

Although it is clear that even when the Dacians were not centralized, they were willing to interfere in Roman-controlled territory, these attacks were low-intensity incursions intended as plundering expeditions, little different from raids by other tribal peoples such as the Germans, the Raetians, the Pannonians or the Sarmatians. These incursions were dealt with in a manner appropriate to their scale, usually amounting to little more than a punitive expedition intended to demonstrate that such behaviour wouldn't be tolerated. As with the Pannonians and Dalmatians, it was not until they joined together for a single cause that the Dacians became a real threat to the Romans. Unfortunately for the Pannonians and Dalmatians, they were not able to carry out their rebellion under the leadership of a single commander or as a united force and lacked the true centralization seen in Dacia under Decebalus. When centralized control was being exerted over Dacia, there is clear evidence that the Dacians were willing to become involved in Roman internal politics, as Burebista had in the civil war between Caesar and Pompey, and posed a much more significant threat to Roman control in the regions south of the Danube including Moesia, Thrace and Macedonia.[7]

The Dacians also possessed a fixed capital at Sarmizegetusa Regia in the Carpathian Mountains (not to be confused with Sarmizegetusa Ulpia, which was the Roman capital of provincial Dacia built in the lowlands by Trajan). Although there can be little doubt about the fact of Dacian centralization, the form it took is particularly interesting in that it was not accompanied by a significant increase in urbanization, which is often used as an indicator of centralization. Even though under central authority, the majority of Dacians still lived in smallholdings, villages and hamlets as they had before, which has led some to question whether it can be argued that the Dacians actually possessed any centralization, particularly during Burebista's reign, but it is too simplistic to assume that centralization can only be demonstrated with accompanying urbanization.

The Dacian fortresses, many of which had been constructed during the reign of Burebista, acted as central points of authority for Decebalus, creating a web which joined the smallholdings and hamlets, if not physically, under the direction of local nobles, who lived in the fortresses and were responsible to the king. This system was copied by the Romans after they had conquered Dacia, their fortresses being situated to function in the same manner as their Dacian predecessors. Although for some time it was believed that the Roman forts were built directly over the top of Dacian sites, it has since been demonstrated by archaeologists that in general terms the Dacian fortresses had been located in the mountains and the Romans fortresses were in the valleys and plains, on new sites corresponding with the new urbanization in the region. Although situated on new sites, the Roman fortresses provided the same centralizing authority their Dacian predecessors had but in terrain more favourable to the Roman military forces.

Fortresses

The cornerstone of the Dacian defensive network was situated in the Oraştie Mountains, in the modern Transylvanian Alps. This consisted of a network of stone fortresses built high in the mountain range. The only fortresses comparable to them are those of the late Iron Age Celts and Gauls but even these lack the planning and execution found in the Dacian fortresses. The network of fortifications in the Oraştie Mountains formed one of the primary focuses of Trajan's Dacian wars. These forts and fortified settlements have benefited from the most archaeological attention, providing us with a firm understanding of many of the architectural and technological features that made these sites important targets for the invading Roman forces.

Three distinctly different types of fortification have been identified in Dacia. The first is the fortified settlement or *dava* which would have been permanently inhabited by the population of a village, a second type can be described as hill forts or citadels which would have been permanently inhabited by a member of the Dacian nobility and his garrison, and the final type is also a fortified hill fort or citadel but this site would have been occupied only on a temporary, as needed, basis.[8] The construction of Dacian fortifications was certainly influenced by those of the Greek colonies on the Black Sea that they encountered during the reign of Burebista, but the Dacian fortifications had unique features not found anywhere else in the Mediterranean world or Europe. They were much more advanced than the earthworks and palisades found in 'barbarian' Europe, and even those in Gaul which Caesar had praised as being difficult to breach even with rams.[9]

Even before the technological advances in wall construction and the use of towers, the Dacians made good use of terrain in order to make their fortifications difficult to assault, placing them in positions where they could exercise dominance over economically-important regions. However, the addition of technological advances in wall design made these fortifications extremely difficult to overcome by any but the most advanced opposition, and their well thought-out placement formed a clear defensive network designed to ensure that opponents could not simply bypass them, but rather were forced to deal with a number of fortifications before they could reach the Dacian capital.

Apart from the *murus Dacicus* or Dacian wall, perhaps the most advanced type of defensive wall in 'barbarian' Europe at the time was the *murus Gallicus* or Gallic wall, which Caesar was confronted with in his Gallic conquest and described in his commentary on the war.[10] The construction of the Gallic wall involved two outer fasciae of rough-hewn stone blocks connected by wooden scaffolding that had been nailed together but with the ends of the beams projecting beyond the stone fascia of the wall. The space between the fasciae around the scaffolding was then filled with compacted *emplekton*.[11] Caesar's discussion of this construction method indicates that this type of wall was impervious to attacks by battering rams as it could absorb much of the shock. The one apparent weakness of this type of wall was the fact that the beams forming the internal scaffolding had their ends exposed and could be set alight, which would significantly weaken the structure.

The wall construction techniques used by the Dacians, however, were a clear advance over the Gallic method and as a result Dacian fortifications were significantly more difficult to overcome. The introduction of the *murus Dacicus* has been dated to the reign of Burebista. Its construction differed from the style of the Gallic wall in a number of ways: firstly, the Dacian wall used larger, dressed rectangular stone blocks for both fasciae of the wall, and at regular intervals blocks had a dovetail joint carved into the top of them into which a stout wooden beam would be slotted connecting the inner and outer fascias of the wall: then like the Gallic wall the space between the fascias was filled with compacted *emplekton*. There is also evidence that these walls were topped with a wooden palisade. These walls would have had the same qualities as the Gallic walls with the addition of protecting the ends of the beams which did not project beyond the outer fascia.

Not all Dacian fortresses had walls constructed in this manner, which has been confirmed both by the archaeological excavations in the region and the reliefs on Trajan's Column which depict at least one example of what has been interpreted as a *murus Gallicus*.[12] In addition to being stronger than the Gallic wall, any fortress protected by the Dacian wall would very likely have been seen as a symbol of very high status. Many Dacian fortresses, in addition to possessing stone walls, made very good use of the steep and inaccessible terrain in the heart of the Carpathians. Additionally, Dacian fortifications were known to make use of ramparts and ditches to hinder the advance of an attacking enemy.

In addition to creating a defensive system for the capital, Dacian fortresses also acted as centres of manufacturing, industry and religion. In order to successfully complete the annexation of Dacia, the Romans were forced to capture several extremely well-defended fortifications, technologically the equal of those produced by the Romans and significantly more advanced than anything else anywhere in Europe at the time. They were also designed to be able to withstand a siege for a prolonged period of time, making excellent use of water and food storage facilities, which are also visible in some of the depictions on Trajan's Column and are evident in the archaeological remains.

There is significant evidence at Sarmizegetusa Regia that very large stores of grain were kept there, as discovered in the remains of burnt granaries at the site. It also seems that there was a connection between the granaries, the metalworking and religious activity at Sarmizegetusa Regia. One suggestion that has been posed is that this indicates some level of involvement by religious leaders in the control of metallurgy, taxation and administration.[13] The choice of location for Sarmizegetusa Regia seems to have rested on a number of important factors: the mountain on which the capital was located was seen as a holy place and as such was important in Dacian religion, the region around Sarmizegetusa Regia was also rich in iron and salt, providing the new Dacian king with some control over these very important resources.

The centralization of industry is in often seen as a hallmark of more advanced societies. Tribal organizations were generally incapable of this,[14] making the Dacians a rather unique proposition for the Romans. Sarmizegetusa Regia displays evidence of significant economic activity, demonstrating its role as a centre of manufacturing.[15] Very large numbers of tools and iron implements have been discovered by archaeologists working at the site.

The Dacian Military

The Dacian army was well-organized, well-trained and well-equipped, and as a result it posed a significant threat to the Roman forces it encountered. Although little is known for certain about the organization of the Dacian army, it seems likely that it employed a tripartite organization, with the highest-ranking *pilleati* acting as commanders, the middle class forming a professional core and the lower class being used to supplement the professionals in wartime.[16]

Having a dedicated officer class and a trained professional core would have gone a long way towards making the Dacian military a very effective fighting force, capable of waging a long-term campaign without facing the difficulties associated with discipline and supply that appear to have been common problems for most barbarian armies. Additionally, there is evidence to suggest that the Dacian soldiers were trained by Roman deserters or military specialists. Such a well-trained, organized and equipped force might have posed a significant threat to the regions around Dacia.

Having been trained in the Roman way of war meant that not only were the Dacians capable of strategic and tactical decisions, they also had a solid understanding of Roman strategy and tactics and as a result understood the conditions preferred by the Roman forces. It is also possible that as a result of the training they received that the Dacian forces were able to conduct advanced battlefield manoeuvres.

A clear hierarchy within the Dacian military is also supported by clearly differing levels of equipment considered the norm for each of these groups. This assessment is supported by Dacian grave finds which assist us in forming a much clearer picture of the arms and armour (panoply) used by various Dacian warriors. Interestingly there are distinct differences in the categories of finds in Dacian graves that have been found to contain military goods (it must also be pointed out that there are far more graves that do not contain military goods than ones that do). Some of the graves actually contained complete panoplies, indicating almost certainly that these graves belonged to members of the elite: a complete panoply found in such a grave could consist of a sword, *sica* (a curved knife), spear, helmet, shield and mail armour. However, even a minimalist approach would indicate that the average Dacian *comati* would be equipped with an oval shield, similar to that of the Roman auxiliaries, and based on evidence from the grave finds possess two melee weapons, most likely a *sica* and a spear, although other combinations are also possible. Taking into consideration the Dacians' resources of iron and their high level of ironworking skill, it seems likely that a far greater percentage of Dacian soldiers were equipped with effective armour and higher-quality weapons than suggested by the minimalist approach, even if this isn't immediately evident in the grave record, which only records what people were willing to bury with the deceased. The enormous number of arrowheads found in the excavations so far also indicates widespread use of the bow and the frequency of horse-related finds including components of tack and harness, suggests a high proportion of Dacian warriors, maybe as many as a third, most likely from the core and command levels of the army, had access to a horse.

One significant aspect of the threat posed by the Dacians to Rome was that they were militarily superior to many of the other peoples that Rome had faced. They were very well supplied with iron and, thanks in part to the Celtic invaders ejected or assimilated during the reign of Burebista, the Dacians possessed skilled craftsmen capable of forging high-quality weapons, armour and equipment which in turn meant that they were able to equip their forces to a standard comparable to the Romans themselves, who are generally considered the best-equipped force in the Mediterranean world of the time.

It is clear that the Dacians were much better equipped than other tribal conglomerations: it has been demonstrated that the average barbarian tribal group during this period was unable to equip a large percentage of their forces with high-quality weaponry. Some modern scholars have estimated that as few as 10 per cent of barbarian warriors could afford a sword, based on an examination of grave finds.[17] The majority of reasonably well-off warriors in this period would be armed with a spear and protected by a shield: this is particularly true of less resource-rich peoples such as the Germans who clearly preferred weapons that required less iron in their construction because of the reduced cost and increased availability. Some Germans who were allies of the Romans during the Dacian wars are depicted on Trajan's Column wielding clubs which are nothing more than tree branches.

The level of equipment Roman soldiers were issued gave them a distinct advantage against their more poorly-equipped opponents. The Roman legionaries of this period were issued with a short sword (the *gladius*) and several javelins (*pila*) and each was equipped with a large rectangular shield (the *scutum*), and protected by high-quality metal armour. This armour could take several forms, the most iconic and technologically-advanced Roman armour being the *lorica segmentata* made up of metal bands, which is the armour that all Roman legionaries are depicted wearing on Trajan's Column. It must be said here that Trajan's Column presents a conventionalized depiction of not only the Dacians but the Roman legionaries as well, illustrating them in the latest iteration of Roman armour although other more realistic representations as depicted on the Adamklissi Monument suggest that many of the older forms of armour, including chain and scale mail, were still in use throughout Trajan's Dacian wars.[18] The high level of equipment issued to every single legionary usually provided Roman forces with a significant advantage against less well-equipped enemies.

However, the Roman equipment advantage was nowhere near as extreme against the Dacians. Unlike many of Rome's other enemies, the Dacians possessed many iron mines that were clearly capable of producing large quantities of high-quality iron in the region. That the Dacians were actively exploiting this resource is confirmed by finds of significant quantities of iron that had been smelted into 'cakes' ready to be worked into a variety of iron implements at Sarmizegetusa Regia. The capital itself appears to have been situated in a very iron-rich region and apparently possessed two terraces devoted specifically to iron working and eight large furnaces. Several hundred iron tools have been discovered on these terraces, indicating a very high level of craft specialization and an organized metal manufacturing industry capable of arming and armouring a large number of Dacian warriors.

That Dacian warriors were better equipped than the average 'barbarian' forces faced by Rome is supported by their depictions on both the monument at Adamklissi and Trajan's Column which clearly indicate that a large proportion of Dacian soldiers were equipped with the native sword, the *falx*. Although the conventionalization of depictions on Trajan's Column needs to be taken into account, the fact that the Adamklissi Monument also depicts almost every Dacian as being equipped with this weapon strongly suggests that it was widely used. The depictions of weapons and armour on the base pedestal of Trajan's Column, in addition to what literary descriptions remain, suggests that Dacian access to quality weapons and armour meant that their force was far better equipped than the Romans might have been accustomed to.

The most iconic Dacian weapon, the *falx* has been the subject of significant debate. The depictions on Trajan's Column and the Adamklissi Monument differ significantly, with the *falx* as depicted on the Column being a short knife-like weapon, whereas the *falx* depicted on both of the Adamklissi Monument and Roman coinage, minted to celebrate Trajan's victory over the Dacians, is a much larger weapon able to be used either one or two-handed.[19] Fronto's description of the vicious wounds inflicted by the *falx* strongly suggest that it could not have been the small knife-like weapon depicted on the Column but rather a longer-handled weapon capable of inflicting serious injuries.[20] This weapon substantially contributed to the significant threat a Dacian warrior posed to a Roman legionary in battle and explains why there are distinct modifications to the Roman armour worn during these wars. The weapon depicted on the Column should more correctly be described as a *sica* which was a curved knife common to the Dacians and the Thracians.

A number of modifications were applied to older forms of Roman armour which predated the introduction of the *lorica segmentata* primarily taking the form of a lengthening of the sleeves and the bottom of the armour. This was achieved by adding a single row of *ptergues* (scales) on the sleeves and a double row at the bottom, to protect the most vulnerable parts of the legionary's body. The Romans also began to reinforce their helmets with previously unseen cross-bracing. The first appearance of this is on a helmet found at Berzobis, which clearly demonstrates that the cross-bracing was a field modification rather than a feature of the helmet's original construction. This is evident because the plume holder, consisting of a brass plate at the top of the helmet, was flattened in order for the cross-bracing to be mounted over the top. Recent tests conducted by the author have demonstrated that the cross-bracing was a very effective addition which helped protect the legionary's head against a downward strike by the Dacian *falx* and specifically lent strength to the apex of the helmet where the metal was generally thinnest due to the techniques used to manufacture Roman helmets.[21]

The widespread depiction of segmented metal arm guards known as *manicae* (singular *manica*) on the Adamklissi Monument further demonstrates the seriousness of the threat a Dacian warrior posed to a Roman legionary.[22] The *manica* consisted of a number of overlapping plates similar in design to *lorica segmentata*. Although there is some recent evidence that suggests that the *manica* was utilized on other fronts against other opponents, it is only during the Dacian wars that it seems to have been in widespread use. Clearly it was introduced to counter the *falx*'s curved blade which was capable of debilitating attacks on the sword arm of a legionary, even bypassing his shield. There is also an argument to be made that the construction of the *manica* used during the Dacian wars differed from that found elsewhere. Those depicted on the Adamklissi monument show the plates overlaping in the opposite direction to those found elsewhere, suggesting that this adaptation was unique to this theatre of conflict, and came about only because of the unique challenges posed by the Dacian *falx*.

Although as yet there is no archaeological evidence to support this theory, it seems unlikely that the soldiers that constructed the Adamklissi Monument were not intimately familiar with this piece of equipment and that they would have made such a fundamental error in its depiction.[23] If the alternate configuration depicted on the Adamklissi Monument is correct, it is likely that it would have provided increased protection against the *falx* unlike the traditional *manica* which it has already been demonstrated allows the *falx* to channel the force of its blow between the protective plates of the arm guard, causing horrific damage to the limb beneath.[24]

In addition to posing a direct threat to the Roman soldiers in the field the Dacian army was one of the more technologically-advanced forces the Romans ever had to face, and certainly the most technologically-advanced 'barbarian' army that the Romans had encountered to date. It is clear that at least by the time of Trajan's wars, unlike typical 'barbarians', the Dacians had access to torsion-powered field artillery.[25] The column provides clear evidence that the Dacians were utilizing *carroballistae* to defend their fortifications. These weapons were also a mainstay of the Roman army: in a scene depicted on Trajan's Column one of these is mounted on the back of a small cart being used by Roman legionaries as field artillery.[26] It was extremely unusual for so-called 'barbarian' peoples to possess such weaponry. Although the simple answer might be to suggest that the Dacians had simply captured these complex weapons from Romans they had previously defeated, this would ignore the fact that in order for these weapons to be used they needed to be regularly tuned and maintained, demonstrating a solid understanding of the principles behind the construction and use of torsion weaponry. It has been suggested that these weapons came into Dacian hands as a result of the engineers lent to Decebalus by Domitian in their peace treaty which is discussed later. This assumption is based solely on the fact that Dio tells us that engineers of every craft including warfare were sent to Decebalus.[27] This does not preclude the possibility that the Dacians had already acquired the capability to use and potentially construct torsion-powered weaponry before their treaty with Domitian: excavations from at least three Dacian fortresses have confirmed the presence of catapult bolt heads dated between the second century BC and the first century AD, increasing the likelihood that the Dacians had access to these technologically-advanced weapons well before the Domitianic treaty. Trajan's Column provides clues to the sort of extraordinary weaponry available to the Dacians. In one scene Trajan is depicted examining a bow and arrow: unfortunately only the arrow still remains, with the bow likely to have been one of the metal components removed from the Column.[28] It has been suggested that the bow Trajan is examining could in fact be a *gastrophetes*, also known as a belly bow, an early form of crossbow. The fact that Trajan is closely examining this bow demonstrates that the weapon is unusual in some way otherwise it would have been unlikely to draw the emperor's attention or have been worthy of depiction on the Column. This, combined with the depiction of a Dacian warrior in a previous scene which also has a missing bow and the way in which he is holding it, lends weight to the argument that the missing weapon may have been a *gastrophetes*.

The Dacians were trained in the art of war by Romans, and as a result they were well prepared and understood how best to fight invaders. In addition to the assistance they received as a result of the treaty with Domitian, Decebalus is known to have taken in Roman deserters who he used to train his own troops in the Roman methods of war: this would have been the case in both Domitian's and Trajan's invasions. This training combined with at least a core of professional soldiers and commanders and previous contact with the Romans ensured that the Dacian monarch had an extremely potent force at his disposal, even though it is likely that it was significantly smaller than the 200,000 troops under Burebista as described by Strabo, and may have been as small as 40,000 troops, which would have still been a substantial force not easily overcome.[29]

The Dacians were capable of attacking Roman fortifications, something relatively unique for a so-called barbarian people. One scene in particular on Trajan's Column illustrates the Dacians actively engaged in besieging a Roman fort.[30] This scene has been described as depicting the Dacian counter-attack in Moesia. The fact that a purportedly 'barbarian' people were engaged in a siege and utilizing siege equipment, in this case a ram, is highly unusual and likely the result of the Romanization of the Dacian army undertaken under the direction of Decebalus and the Roman deserters or engineers.

Many modern authors seem to believe that the Dacian forces wore no armour at all, based on the conventionalized depictions of Dacian troops found on Trajan's Column, where they are depicted as solely relying on their shields for protection. These shields, identical to those carried by the Roman auxiliaries, differed only in the designs on the front. Strobel sensibly argues that it would be nearly unbelievable to think that after hundreds of years of contact with the Celts, Greeks, Sarmatians, and Romans that the Dacians would not have adopted some form of body armour.[31] Excavations of some graves dated to the period before the Dacian wars demonstrates that some Dacians possessed chain mail armour: additionally there is evidence of a small quantity of bronze scales being found in a number of graves. This last find suggests that the scales formed reinforced portions of the armour worn by the Dacian interred, possibly fastened to an organic backing, like leather, which has deteriorated over time leaving no trace.

Add to this the fact that the Dacians were blessed with an abundance of iron in their region and their obvious skill in working it make the argument that they did not equip themselves with effective armour seem even less plausible. The base of Trajan's Column provides additional evidence for the use of armour not seen in the scenes themselves. The depictions on the base, referred to as the *congeries armorum* depict helmets and various types of armour including scale and chain mail. Similarly, a detailed examination of the Adamklissi Monument goes some way towards confirming armour use by the Dacians, albeit to a limited extent. The metopes on the Adamklissi Monument present evidence of the Dacian use of helmets. Further confirmation can be found on the Trajanic coins minted to celebrate the Roman victory which again illustrate Dacian armour use.[32] Although it is impossible to say exactly how widespread the use of armour was amongst the Dacian forces, a safe assumption would be that at least many of the commanders and possibly the professional core of the army had access to and wore quality metal armour.

The renewed unification of the Dacian tribes under Decebalus sometime in or about the time of Domitian's reign, combined with their high levels of training and professionalism, their well-constructed and situated fortifications and their access to high-quality weapons and armour made the Dacians a force to be reckoned with, even by the seemingly invincible Romans.

Chapter 7

The Flavian Danube

During the period of the Flavian emperors the Danube again became a very active region. Vespasian, the first of the Flavian emperors, took control of Rome after his victory during the 'Year of Four Emperors', AD 69. Before the new emperor was even able to make his way back to Rome some Dacians intent on taking advantage of the weakened frontier had crossed the Danube. The Flavians faced a number of opponents from across the Danube during their reigns: Sarmatian tribes, the Suebic Marcomanni and the Dacians. The Danube clearly became a focal area for approximately the next four decades.

During the civil wars of AD 69 the people of the Danube again demonstrated their troublesome nature to Rome. Nine thousand Sarmatian Roxolani had taken advantage of the fact that Rome was engaged in a civil war over who would rule after Nero, and crossed the Danube, invading Moesia in the short period that Otho was emperor but before the Illyrian legions had become actively involved in the civil war on the side of Vespasian. The Roxolani may well have been encouraged by the fact that they had defeated two cohorts of Roman troops the previous winter, and felt that while the attention of Rome was focused inward they had an opportunity to gain significant plunder in Moesia. Tacitus's record illustrates that the Roxolani were more interested in looting than in actual fighting and that they certainly were not interested in territorial expansion.[1] As a result the Roxolani forces became somewhat dispersed looking for booty and heavily encumbered as a result of how much they had collected, making it difficult for them to fight the Roman forces when they were engaged by them.

The Romans also had luck on their side as the winter snow was melting, making footing for the Sarmatian horses difficult and thereby taking the prime Roxolani weapon away from them. The Roxolani were not accustomed to fighting on foot, their speciality being fighting from horseback using a long lance or sword, weapons that were not easily adapted to an infantry engagement against Roman forces. Normally the heavily-armoured Sarmatians, using the speed of their horses and the length of their weapons, would charge enemy infantry formations, Tacitus saying that hardly any line could resist charging Roxolani horsemen.[2] As heavily armoured as they were, in either scale or mail armour, the Roxolani did not use shields, a major weakness when, as they were in this case, forced to fight on foot against an infantry army like the Romans. Only a few Sarmatians managed to escape the Roman forces and they are said to have hidden themselves in nearby swamps where they died either due to the cold or from wounds sustained in the fighting.

As the victor in the Year of Four Emperors, Vespasian has naturally received significant attention on his early career, his victory in the civil war and to the reforms he implemented after his victory, particularly his economic policies. However, little attention has been paid to his actions along the Danubian frontier. Vespasian's reign saw significant activity in Raetia, Pannonia and Moesia, illustrating a shift in frontier policy and an increase in the importance placed on defending the Danube frontier relative to the other northern frontier, the Rhine. Vespasian was a man with a great deal of military experience. During the reign of Claudius he had commanded a legion in Germany and had fought thirty battles in Britain where Suetonius tells us that he subdued two tribes and captured more than twenty towns. His success in Britain earned him triumphal decorations, two priesthoods and a two-month term as consul as rewards.[3]

Vespasian's military career continued even after a falling-out with Nero the last of the Julio-Claudian emperors, who recalled him to active service and tasked him with suppressing a Jewish rebellion.[4] It appears that Vespasian was chosen not only because of his obscure background which did not lend itself to Imperial pretensions, but more importantly because of his military skill. Nero supplied him with two legions, eight cavalry squadrons, and ten auxiliary cohorts, which he added to the troops already stationed in Judaea. Vespasian was still actively engaged in the fighting in Judaea when Nero died and civil war broke out to determine control of Rome.[5]

After the year-long civil war that saw the defeat and death of three other claimants to the throne, Vespasian became emperor in the year AD 69. His victory was largely a result of the military support he received from the legions stationed in the provinces and it is possible that he may not even have challenged for the position had it not been for the request he received from a significant number of men based within the three legions in Moesia. These troops, which had originally declared for Otho, feared that after his death they would be severely punished by Vitellius, his immediate successor, so offered their support to Vespasian. After receiving the soldiers' request for assistance, Vespasian chose to declare for the principate. Needless to say, the legions he was commanding in Judaea also supported his claim to the throne, as did several foreign rulers including the Parthian king Vologaesus, who offered Vespasian the use of 40,000 of his archers.[6]

Interestingly, the support Vespasian received from the Moesian legions led to increased pressure on the Danubian frontier. Trouble on this frontier started before Vespasian was even able to claim Imperial authority, with the troublesome Dacians crossing the Danube in order to take advantage of the civil war and the resulting reduction in troop numbers guarding the border, possibly with the intention of reclaiming control of Moesia for themselves.[7]

The Moesian legionaries having departed to press Vespasian's claim to the throne, only auxiliary units and the river fleets were left to defend the frontier. The Dacians did not act at first but once they realized the extent of the Roman civil war crossed the Danube and attacked the remaining Roman auxiliary forces and took control of both banks of the river.[8] Only the fortuitous arrival of Vespasian's ally Mucianus, who was marching on Rome in his support, and the hard work of the Pannonian and Moesian fleets saw the Dacians forced back. Tacitus tells us that because Mucianus feared the possibility of both the Germans and the Dacians attacking the Empire as a result of the civil war, and having received word of the Moesian legionaries' victory at Cremona against the forces of Vitellius, felt he needed divert his forces to deal with the Dacian incursion.[9] The Pannonian and Moesian river fleets had apparently performed extremely well in defending the Empire from the Dacians and were awarded the title *Flavia* for this and their support of the new emperor.[10]

Vespasian had a strong connection to the Danube throughout his entire life. Interestingly he was born in the year AD 9, the same year that saw the end of the Pannonian rebellion.[11] Vespasian was responsible for a number of changes on this frontier: it seems that the establishment of naval bases in Pannonia, Moesia and Rhaetia were a result of his reforms. Recent archaeological discoveries have also demonstrated that Vespasian significantly strengthened the Danubian defences during his reign. This did not equate to Vespasian actually increasing the number of troops deployed on the frontier, rather he redeployed them and changed the tactical focus from one of cavalry to infantry. New work was undertaken at Carnuntum and at Aquinicum, the latter being located directly opposite the Sarmatian Iazyges at a point where the Danube could be forded and, in an effort to secure the fastest route to the lower Danube, Vespasian set up Roman colonies at either end of the Save River at Segestica and Sirmium.

Domitian

> The Sarmatians and Suebi rose against us; the Dacians won fame by defeats inflicted and suffered; even the Parthians were almost aroused to arms.
>
> Tac., *Hist* 1.2.

After Vespasian's death his eldest son Titus became emperor, but he did not live long, ruling for only about two years.[12] He was succeeded by his younger brother Domitian, who became one of the most maligned and hated emperors in Roman history. Upon assuming the principate, Domitian continued his father's policies when it came to the Danubian frontier. As well as strengthening the defences in general, he paid particular attention to any potential river crossings.

In his very short reign before dying of illness, Titus had two major disasters to contend with, including the eruption of Vesuvius, which would have kept him well occupied. There was no action to speak of on the Danube during his reign. Like his father, Titus was an experienced military commander, with victories in Judaea, but his younger brother Domitian had no such record. Domitian has been accused of engaging in unnecessary campaigns in the hope of earning the military reputation that he clearly desired. Almost immediately after Vespasian had taken control in Rome, Domitian is said to have petitioned his father to allow him to engage in a German war. Vespasian did not allow this, and provided him no opportunities to earn the military experience he craved.

Domitian is the victim of hostile sources that present all his actions in the most unfavourable light possible. An excellent example of this is the way that his Dacian war is described and how the results of this conflict are presented. In fact it can be argued that this is also the series of events most likely to rehabilitate our view of Domitian, as close examination of what occurred demonstrates that his actions were very similar to those of Trajan, who was glorified for the way in which he handled his Dacian Wars, whereas Domitian was roundly criticized in the sources for his efforts. However, Domitian was the first emperor to spend a substantial part of his reign away from Rome personally involved in military campaigns.[13]

Similarly, Domitian was heavily criticized for his war against the Chatti, a German people who lived east of the Rhine. His war against them in AD 83 has been described as a nothing more than a sham victory. He is accused by Tacitus of enhancing, or even outright falsifying, his success against the Germans, saying he dressed slaves as Germans and taught them to speak the language, so that they could be made to march in his triumphal celebrations as the defeated enemy in an effort to make it appear like he had conquered these people when in fact he hadn't even come in contact with them.[14] There are indications in other ancient sources that suggest that although there was certainly an element of duplicity in what Domitian did to the Chatti, there may also have been a genuine victory to be celebrated. Again the bias in the sources is evident and needs to be taken into account, as Tacitus was particularly anti-Domitian, since his father-in-law was Agricola, the Roman commander in Britain under Domitian. Domitian had ordered the withdrawl of legions from Britain for the emperor's own use, and had recalled Agricola in AD 85, according to Tacitus, out of jealousy because of his successes which outshone Domitian's military achievements.

Unlike many of the other sources, Frontinus suggests that Domitian's campaign against the Chatti was actually quite successful. Domitian's forces advanced along a front almost 200km wide in an effort to prevent the Chatti from being able to disappear into the woods as had so often happened when the Romans fought the Germans. Frontinus tells us that this not only changed the nature of the war but forced the enemy from their hiding places and thereby increased the security of the frontier.[15] Suetonius suggests that Domitian's war against the Chatti was completely unjustified, as they had a peace treaty with Rome and as such should never have been attacked.[16] There is no evidence in any of the sources that the Chatti had in any way broken their treaty with Rome, indicating that the reason for Domitian's war against them needs to be found elsewhere. Domitian's advance to the front was conducted in such a way that the enemy could not determine the Romans' intentions. The Emperor made his way to the front, without attracting undue concern on the part of the Chatti, by explaining that his presence was so that Rome could conduct a census of Gaul. This was a plausible explanation and combined with the fact that the Chatti thought they were at peace with Rome, ensured that they were taken completely by surprise.

The cause of Domitian's apparently unnecessary militarism against the Chatti has been traced back to his desire for a German war to match his brother Titus's achievements in the East. Additionally, the fact that Domitian was one of the few emperors to date who had come to the throne with no military experience prior to becoming *princeps* would have certainly added to his desire to demonstrate that he too could be a successful military commander.

The war against the Chatti provided Domitian with his only experience of military command before matters on the Danube reignited and became more serious than ever before. The province of Moesia remained a trouble-spot with low-intensity incursions and raids by the Dacians at any time the frontier looked vulnerable, and was again invaded in AD 85. The Dacians mounted what can only be seen as a significant incursion into Moesia, where they engaged with and killed many Roman troops before also killing the governor, Oppius Sabinus.[17] In AD 84 Sabinus been co-consul with Domitian, and this sort of incursion into the Empire and more importantly still the killing of a Roman governor could not be left unchecked requiring a strong military response particularly as the Dacians had raided Roman territory in Moesia in AD 6 when the Governor of Moesia rushed to the aid of the Romans in Pannonia during the rebellion there but was forced to return less than a year later in AD 7 in order to expel the Dacians who had crossed the Danube. The Dacians had again crossed into Moesia at the end of the Year of Four Emperors, showing that they were ready to pounce on any sign of weakness along the frontier.

Rome could not afford for her enemies to get any hint of weakness on the frontier and decide that they could begin raiding Roman territory. This was particularly true on a frontier that had as many enemies along it as the Danube. It had to be defended against Germans, Dacians and several Sarmatian tribes, all of which were capable of applying pressure on the Roman defences. It is important to note that at this point there were no Roman legions stationed on the Danube east of Novae.[18] Therefore, the troops stationed between Novae and the mouth of the Danube were scattered detachments of auxiliaries and the Moesian fleet established by Vespasian. The other possibility that had to be considered was the potential that any significant signs of weakness could lead to all of the northern peoples seizing the opportunity to cross the frontier at the same time, a circumstance that the Romans would not have been able to deal with.

It is clear that several attempts had been made to deal with the Dacians over a prolonged period of time, Caesar proposed an expedition against them but was assassinated before he was able to undertake it, Augustus claimed to have defeated several Dacian kings and claimed to have subdued the Dacians forcing them to adhere to the will of Rome this was at the very least an exaggeration and although he may have cowed some of the Dacian tribes during his reign the effect of his punitive action did not last and the Dacians were far from pliable or subdued by the time of Domitian's principate.

The Dacian Raid into Moesia

The Roman system of frontier defence devised by Augustus was limited by the number of legionary and auxiliary forces available. Augustus had halved the number of post-civil war legions from its height of sixty to what became Rome's normal complement of about thirty, as the expense of maintaining sixty legions was too heavy a burden for the Roman *fiscus* to maintain. This reduction saw the armies of Rome mostly posted in the frontier provinces, which did not allow for any significant strategic reserve or any in-depth defence of the Empire. This is clearly demonstrated by the need to remove detachments of soldiers from provinces that were relatively peaceful every time Rome became involved in a significant conflict. This was a problem for Domitian, who wanted matters in Britain resolved so that he would be able to immediately free at least one of the British legions for service on the Danube.[19] That Agricola did not finish the campaign within the expected time presented Domitian with difficulties in raising the number of troops he felt were required for his other campaigns. In order to raise the troops he needed Domitian removed vexillations (detachments) from each of the four legions at Agricola's disposal, thus weakening his forces in Britain because he required them in Germany and Moesia.[20]

Therefore, any invasion into Roman territory could become a very serious matter. The defensive system orchestrated by Augustus relied on a forward defence, with Roman forces moving beyond the frontiers to intercept an enemy before they could actually do any damage to the Empire itself. Unfortunately, this type of system could account for every possible incursion and a fast-moving enemy was likely to be able to make it across the border and attack Roman provinces. This is seen in several cases throughout the Empire, and the Dacian raid into Moesia that led to Domitian's Dacian war was a prime example.

In the years between the reign of Tiberius and that of Domitian, the Dacians had posed no significant threat as they lacked the political unity they had possessed under Burebista and would achieve again under Decebalus. The crossing of the Danube was an audacious move by the Dacian king and was bound to attract a Roman response, leaving the Emperor very little choice but to engage in a serious punitive expedition. Even Suetonius, who accuses Domitian of engaging in unprovoked campaigns, readily admits that his Dacian war was not one of them.[21] The Dacian raid took the Roman garrison in Moesia by complete surprise. Jordanes tells us that the Dacians crossed the Danube and laid waste to the Roman side of the river. The Roman Governor of Moesia, Oppius Sabinus, marched against the invaders immediately with the V *Macedonica* legion which was based at Oescus. However, Sabinus and his troops were defeated by the invaders in the winter of AD 85, the Roman governor himself being killed and the V *Macedonica* seriously mauled and forced to fall back.[22] The IIII *Flavia* legion and numerous auxiliaries were rushed from Dalmatia to Moesia but by the time they arrived Diurpaneus, who later was renamed Decebalus (the orchestrator of the second Dacian unification), had already sacked several cities and towns and had taken many Romans prisoner. Domitian had very little choice other than to deal with the Dacian problem decisively.

The Dacians began their second period of unification under a new king. Their reunification under Decebalus saw them re-emerge as a significant threat to Roman frontier defence on the Danube. Strabo, the geographer, suggested that the Dacians had previously had a force of 200,000 men at the time of Burebista's reign, but it seems that this large force was no longer available to Decebalus, who had taken over as the Dacian monarch after Duras willingly abdicated in his favour because he believed him to be a better military leader.[23] The Dacians needed the best military commander available with the Romans planning a major punitive expedition against them. Decebalus is said to have had access to approximately 40,000 troops, which was still a very large force capable of threatening the Roman hold on Moesia if that was what the Dacians decided to do.

Unlike many of the emperors before him. Domitian did actually make his way to the frontier and was physically near, if not directly involved in, the operations of AD 82/3, 85, 86 and 89. Although most probably based in Moesia during the Dacian wars, he is accused of spending this time carousing and drinking rather than leading the military campaign in person as Trajan was to do later.[24] However, it is quite possible that these allegations are nothing more than another example of anti-Domitianic propaganda, which used the actions of Trajan to make Domitian appear even worse.

Although it is true that he left the command of the Roman forces in the hands of his generals, this had been done by popular emperors like Augustus who are not criticized by the sources for not leading the legions themselves. Many of the criticisms levelled against Domitian must be considered in light of how they present the Emperor Trajan. Trajan was the first real warrior emperor to lead his troops into battle from the front for some time, so in order to emphasize this fact sources friendly to Trajan ensured that they denigrated Domitian for not doing the same thing. Similarly, Domitian's treaty with the Dacian King is roundly criticized even though it was not substantially different to that brokered by Trajan at the end of his first Dacian war.[25]

Domitian's Dacian war illustrates the threat a united barbarian force posed to Rome and explicitly demonstrates the threat the Dacians themselves posed to the Roman army. This war illustrates Decebalus's tactics against the Roman forces, the intelligence of the Dacian leadership and perhaps just as importantly the overconfidence of the Romans. Perhaps the most important threat to emerge as a result of the success seen by the Dacian forces was the potential for the formation of an anti-Roman alliance. Any such alliance formed by Roman enemies along this frontier could have been absolutely disastrous for the Empire. Any continued Dacian success could just have encouraged other peoples along the Danube to attack Roman territory. If several of the larger groups launched attacks simultaneously along this frontier they would have stretched Roman defensive capabilities if not beyond their limits then certainly to them. To some degree the evidence of this is reflected in Domitian's hurried departure from Dacia, in order to deal with an emerging threat elsewhere, which clearly suggests that the Roman forces at this time were unable to deal with multiple threats along the frontier, particularly after the reduction in the number of legions by Augustus.

It has been argued that the most efficient solution to the problems in this region would have been a secure system of client kingships supported by the payment of financial subsidies, as annexation was a very expensive option.[26] In addition to the costs of mounting a campaign of annexation the maintenance of a newly-annexed province in terms of troops and infrastructure was exceptionally high. Seen in this light, the terms reached by Domitian with Decebalus were a sensible, efficient and reasonable solution.

Domitian's First Attack on Dacia

Domitian, accompanied by the praetorian prefect Cornelius Fuscus, marched to Moesia and set up headquarters at Naissus. Dio tells us that in Moesia Domitian was busy drinking and engaging in lewd behaviour with women and boys alike.[27] Other sources, however, give a very different view of Domitian's campaigns and his leadership. Frontinus tells us that a significant amount of road-building took place, totalling about 75km-worth, which suggests a well-planned advance.[28] He is also said to have reimbursed those whose property was damaged by his army.[29] The fact that Domitian accompanied the Roman forces as far as Moesia demonstrates that at the very least he wished to be associated with a victory against the Dacians. If the descriptions of his conduct whilst in the region are purely the result of an anti-Domitianic tradition that is clearly visible in the sources, the chances are that although not at the front himself he was orchestrating operations from the rear. Interestingly, this emperor appears in a scene in Juvenal's sixteen satires before departing for Moesia.[30] In the satire he is said to have called together his advisers in order to determine what is to be done with a large fish that he had been given. Three of the advisers named by the author, Pegasus, Rubrius Gallus, and Cornelius Fuscus, are men who can be shown to have had experience on the Danube or near Dacia. Pegasus had governed Dalmatia, Rubrius Gallus had fought against the Sarmatians after they had killed the Moesian governor Fonteius Agrippa who was succeeded by Oppius Sabinus, and the third was Cornelius Fuscus who had been procurator of Pannonia. There is also a fourth *amici* mentioned by Juvenal, Pompeius although his precise identity is uncertain. If this is Marcus Pompeius Silvanus Staberius Flavinus, then he too had governed Dalmatia.[31] This suggests that although this author was attempting to make Domitian look foolish, there is a case to be made that he had called on advisers with knowledge of this theatre of operations and consulted with them before launching an assault against Dacia, which would paint Domitian in a very different light and may well suggest that his actions were logical and those of any good commander before leading his forces to battle.

Apparently Decebalus sent several envoys to Domitian requesting a truce so that Rome and Dacia could return to peaceful relations, but Domitian repeatedly rejected these overtures, since accepting these would certainly have made the Emperor and Rome look weak in the eyes of the Dacians and their neighbours. After the Dacian raid into Roman territory and the killing of a Roman official, a military response was essential.

Domitian's use of generals to directly command the Roman forces is undeniable. The first general he used against the Dacians was Cornelius Fuscus, a man of equestrian rank who had been the prefect of Domitian's Praetorian Guard since AD 81, was given supreme control of the war against them.[32] He was sent against the Dacians with a large force sometime in the year AD 85. Fuscus, at the head of the five legions, initially met with some success and was able to expel the Dacians from Moesia. Domitian seems to have returned to Rome after these initial successes apparently celebrating a double triumph, for his victory against the Chatti in AD 83 and for pushing the Dacians out of Moesia.[33]

But the Dacian forces were not to be that easily defeated as Decebalus was an extremely intelligent commander and he himself was in command. Furthermore, Decebalus had prepared his forces to face the Romans by hiring Roman deserters to train them in the Roman way of war. Dio tells us that when Decebalus learnt that the Emperor had sent an army against him, he sent another envoy to Domitian offering the Emperor peace if every Roman paid Decebalus two obols per year.[34]

Domitian remained in Rome in the first half of the following year.[35] It was during this period that Cornelius Fuscus, who was not renowned for his patience, crossed the Danube in pursuit of the Dacians to avenge the death of Oppius Sabinus and win more glory for Rome. He crossed the Danube by means of the bridge of boats,[36] but it appears that the Roman advance into Dacia was largely uncontested and that the lowland regions had been abandoned by the Dacians in favour of their fortresses located in the mountains. This is a tactic that they used again against Trajan and is clearly based on an understanding of the Roman army and that the legionary forces were best suited to large-scale combat on an open plain. Therefore, by not engaging the Roman forces in terrain suited to them, the Dacian king was effectively improving his chances against the Romans. The suggestion made by Dio that Decebalus had a very solid understanding of warfare and was an expert in ambushes as well as pitched battles is clearly demonstrated by the tactics he chose to employ against the Romans. The site of the engagement with the forces of Cornelius Fuscus was located in the Orăştie mountains, possibly near Tapae.

As there is no clear evidence that allows us to determine the exact location of Tapae, there are still significant debates over its location, with one recent author suggesting that it was located in the Muresh Valley north of the Orăştie mountains and the more traditional view suggests that Tapae was located somewhere near the pass known as the Iron Gates. This was a narrow 15km-long passage which formed a formidable obstacle in its natural state, made more so by the Dacian addition earthen defence works.

Unfortunately for the Romans Decebalus, having drawn them into terrain more suited to the Dacians, was well-prepared and ambushed Fuscus and his forces, killing the Roman commander and wiping out *Legio* V *Alaudae*. The Dacians captured the Roman standards and their war machines and Jordanes tells us that they plundered the soldiers' camp of all its wealth.[37] It was not until the reign of Trajan that the standards lost here were to be retrieved. The loss of the Moesian Governor and an entire legion was a significant blow to the Romans.

The surviving Roman forces made their way back across the Danube into Moesia and let Domitian, who had returned to the front some time about August AD 86, know the results of the engagement. Dio tells us that the troops who had survived this encounter with Decebalus and made their way back to Moesia asked Domitian to lead them. However, one of his first acts was to divide the province of Moesia into Moesia Superior and Moesia Inferior. Additionally Domitian strengthened the Moesian garrison he did this by moving three legions to the Danube: III *Flavia* from Dalmatia to Moesia Superior, I *Adiutrix* from Germany to Sirmium, and II *Adiutrix* from Britain also to Sirmium. The fact that he was willing to weaken two other major frontiers, Germany and Britain, demonstrates the seriousness of the threat posed by the Dacians. Domitian then returned to Rome in order to prepare for a second punitive campaign against Dacia. Domitian left Nigrinus, who he had appointed Governor of Moesia after Sabinus's death, in charge of Moesia Inferior which was the part of the province located furthest east. He then brought Vettonianus from Pannonia to take command of Moesia Superior. Vettonianus had had significant experience on the Danube being stationed in Dalmatia and Pannonia, before he was moved to upper Moesia by the time he was replaced by Tettius Julianus who had spent approximately eight years in the region.

Although there are no details available to us, these two commanders apparently had managed to achieve some successes against the Dacians in AD 86 as both received substantial military awards and Domitian received his 13th and 14th salutations as *imperator* late the same year.

Domitian's Second Attack on Dacia

AD 87 saw no further action on the Danube, Tettius Julianus was appointed Governor of Moesia Superior, replacing Vettonianus. Julianus had been consul in AD 83 and had demonstrable experience on the Danube.[38] He had commanded the VII *Claudia* legion and defeated the Roxolani in AD 69. Julianus is further mentioned in Tacitus's *Histories* in relation to the Year of Four Emperors and a plot to assassinate him initiated by the then Governor of Moesia, Aponius Saturninus, who sent a centurion to kill Julianus. Having learnt of the plot, Julianus escaped into the Balkan Mountains with some of his men. Although he discussed supporting Vespasian in the civil war this never actually happened.

Julianus had a reputation as a strict disciplinarian,[39] which was exactly what was needed after the impetuous nature of Fuscus which led to a significant Roman defeat. Domitian's second attack against Dacia occurred in AD 88 under the command of the new Governor of Moesia Superior, the general Tettius Julianus. The Roman forces first went to Viminacium across the Banat to the Iron Gates in an effort to reach the Dacian capital of Sarmizegetusa Regia and Decebalus. However, late in the year the second campaign against the Dacians concluded with a battle at Tapae, where the Romans defeated the Dacian forces but the onset of winter prevented the Romans pushing on to the Dacian capital. Trying to move the Roman forces through the heavily-fortified Carpathians in winter would almost certainly have resulted in severe losses.

Tapae was a location favoured by Decebalus, as we can see by the number of battles against the Romans he fought there. He clearly thought that it suited the Dacian army more than the Roman legions as it was terrain was mountainous and heavily forested. The location itself was extremely important to the Dacians as it guarded the entry to the string of fortifications in the Orăştie mountains which in turn protected Sarmizegetusa Regia. This site was used again during Trajan's first Dacian war.

The German Situation

January AD 89 saw Domitian's troubles further compounded when the Governor of Upper Germany, Lucius Antonius Saturninus, rose in revolt against him. Saturninus funded his revolt by seizing the treasuries of two of the German legions.[40] It has been suggested that Domitian was considering returning to Dacia to see the war there brought to a conclusion, possibly with the capture of Sarmizegetusa Regia, but Saturninus's revolt would have forced the Emperor to put this on hold at least for the time being. Domitian sent the Governor of Lower Germany, Lappius Maximus, the procurator of Raetia and the future emperor Trajan, who was at the time based in Spain, to deal with the revolt in upper Germania. The revolt was very short-lived, lasting only twenty-four days, but it could have been much worse had an unexpected thaw not prevented the German tribes, including the Chatti, which Saturninus had come to an agreement with from lending him their assistance. Although over quickly, this revolt interrupted Domitian's campaign against the Dacians and very likely encouraged him to make terms with the Dacian King, who was still at large at the beginning of AD 89.

The Chatti

In the same year as Saturninus's revolt, Domitian became involved in a war against the Chatti and another Pannonian war. Whilst on the German front, Domitian decided to engage the Chatti who had come into conflict with Rome as recently as AD 83 when the Emperor had failed to completely conquer them. Although Tacitus in the *Germania* makes it clear that this particular tribe was more of a threat than many of the tribes that Rome had encountered, Tacitus describes the Chatti as being able to think and behave tactically, follow orders and exhibit Roman-like discipline.[41] This is not, however, demonstrated in the events of AD 89 where their involvement in Saturninus's revolt was limited by the unexpected thaw of the Rhine and only led to the destruction of some of the Roman frontier defences. The Governor of Lower Germany, Lappius Maximus, who had come to Domitian's assistance against Saturninus, was sent against the Chatti and seemingly defeated them without too much difficulty.

Domitian's First Pannonian War

According to Cassius Dio, the Emperor himself was responsible for the outbreak of his Pannonian war as he attacked the Suebi and the Quadi because they had refused to provide him with help against the Dacians. Furthermore, Dio tells us that Domitian rejected both of the German attempts to sue for peace, going so far as to execute members of the second embassy.[42] Again, the details of this war are obscure and the actual events of the first phase are extremely difficult to determine. However, what we do know is that early on the Suebian Marcomanni defeated Domitian's forces. Knowing that he did not want to be involved in a war on two fronts at this point, Domitian sought to make peace with the Dacians and brokered a treaty with the Dacians that drew significant criticism. Domitian's approach to dealing with the Germans changed after the defeat and focused on diplomatic relations with the peoples around the Suebian Marcomanni, in an effort to isolate them by surrounding them with hostile neighbours loyal to Rome.

The Dacian Treaty and Reactions to It

The settlement with Dacia, although not popular in the sources and probably not popular with the generals at the time, was sold to the wider public as a victory and certainly did minimize the possibility that Rome would be engaged in a war on two fronts. The Pannonian war of AD 89 was so serious that even though it seemed that the Dacians were on the back foot and likely to have been defeated in the not-too-distant future Domitian felt the need to urgently come to terms with Decebalus. The treaty struck with the Dacians and Decebalus, which has been roundly criticized by the ancient sources and many modern writers, included a large financial payment to Decebalus and continuing financial stipends paid annually, the supply of Roman technical experts, and Decebalus was made a client King of Rome, most likely with the intention of using Dacia as a buffer zone between the Roman provinces located south of the Danube and the peoples on the other side of the river. Rather than going to Rome himself, Decebalus sent a member of the royal family, Diegis, to Rome to accept the crown from Domitian rather than turning up himself, a further insult to Rome which was probably a very wise idea considering how the Romans probably felt about him. The defeat of the Chatti in AD 89 and the settlement with the Dacians in the same year allowed Domitian to return to Rome by November of that year and celebrate a double triumph over these two people.[43]

The Second Pannonian War (AD 92)

The second Pannonian war started because the Lygians, a people living north of Moesia, had come under attack from the Marcomannic Suebi and sent an envoy to Domitian asking for assistance. Domitian decided to send 100 knights to assist the Lygians against the Suebi, a very small force for the purpose. The Suebi, angered by the fact that Domitian had sent assistance to their enemies, allied themselves with the Sarmatian Iazyges against Rome.[44] The Iazyges lived in the plains in the western part of Dacia adjacent to the Danube. Because Domitian had come to terms with Decebalus, the Roman forces sent against the Iazyges and their allies were able to march through Dacia unmolested by the Dacians and attack the Sarmatian Iazyges from the rear, which would have proved a significant advantage.

Domitian sent in an advance force against the Iazyges, which was led by Velius Rufus. Again little detail is available for what actually occurred but the Sarmatians defeated the Romans and apparently destroyed an entire legion, XXI *Rapax*. This war lasted approximately eight months, ending in a Roman victory, but as is so often the case in this region there are no real details available. That there might have been a third Pannonian war is suggested and debated with some evidence pointing towards the possibility that one occurred late in Domitian's reign possibly between AD 95 and 96 the evidence however is far from conclusive some of which could also be dated to the reign of Vespasian.

Roman forces in upper Moesia and Pannonia had been substantially increased since the early 90s AD. In the last years of Domitian's reign five legions were stationed in Pannonia and numerous auxiliaries were stationed in upper Moesia, clearly demonstrating that matters on the Danubian front were far from settled.

Much of Domitian's reign was spent fighting on or near the Danubian frontier. He would not be the only emperor to spend a significant part of his principate on this frontier but he was the first. It is particularly interesting that the times when the Dacians proved to be the most problematic to Rome coincide with the times that Dacia was unified under the leadership of a single king. During the reign of Caesar this was Burebista and the Dacians proved willing to interfere in the Roman civil war. Under Domitian, Decebalus came to the fore and the Dacians again demonstrated a willingness to interpose themselves in Roman territory. It was the events in Moesia that prompted Domitian to retaliate against the Dacians and initiate the war of AD 85 to 86. The reversals suffered during this war went a long way towards demonstrating the threat posed by the Dacians particularly when unified under the leadership of a single militarily-skilled king. It seems likely that Domitian had planned to resolve the Dacian problem but matters with the Germans meant he had to change focus. A somewhat more generous reading of events than that provided by the sources might argue that Domitian's actions against the Germans were a necessary precursor to another war against the Dacians. Unfortunately for this emperor, however, the conclusion of the Dacian war with a treaty between Rome and Decebalus which could not be revisited before his death saw Domitian roundly criticized after his demise, with accusations that the settlement entered into was effectively a bribe paying the Dacians for peace and to pretend they had been defeated. The fact that Domitian was not able to complete the defeat of the Dacians provided Trajan with a clear way to differentiate himself from this very unpopular emperor. Furthermore, Domitian's perceived failure provided him with the perfect opportunity to demonstrate his military prowess and to return to expansionistic rule. Pliny, possibly one of Trajan's most enthusiastic supporters, utilized his successes against the Dacians as a clear counterpoint to what he saw as Domitian's failure describing what happened at the end of Domitian's campaigns in an extremely unflattering light.[45]

The criticism of Domitian can be considered somewhat excessive, as it can just as easily be argued that the Emperor had more pressing matters to deal with elsewhere and a rapid resolution with Decebalus was strategically important as it freed up resources so that the more urgent matters on the German frontier could be dealt with in a timely fashion before a return to Dacia where things might have been settled in a more acceptable manner. Domitian had rejected expansionist warfare in both Germany and Britain to the disappointment of his general staff,[46] but he had faced three dangerous opponents on the Danube during his reign, the Sarmatians, the Marcomanni and the Dacians, and managed to maintain the overall integrity of the Danubian frontier.

Chapter 8

Trajan's Dacian Wars

Trajan had been a general during the reign of Domitian and his successor Nerva. The aged Nerva had been selected by the Senate to replace the despised Domitian but suffered from being extremely unpopular with the one group in Roman society that actually appreciated Domitian whilst he was *princeps*, the army. Pliny actually tells of:

> The great blot on our age, the deadly wound inflicted on our realm, was the time when an emperor and father of the human race was besieged in his palace, arrested and confined . . . A ruler was forced to put men to death against his will.
>
> Pliny, VI.1.

Nerva found himself in an untenable position, clearly unable to hold on to imperial authority without the support of the army. His position was further weakened because he possessed no clear successor. Nerva therefore chose to adopt Trajan in AD 97. His choice was based on a number of factors, not the least of which included the fact that Trajan was a very well-respected military commander acceptable to both the army and the Senate, as is demonstrated by the fact that his appointment immediately put an end to the discord between the army and Nerva and seems to have been a universally popular choice.[1] Nerva announced the adoption when Trajan sent the Emperor word of his successful completion of a campaign in Pannonia, probably against the Suebic Marcomanni. Trajan was sent to take command of the army in Germany, providing him with a very significant military force close to Rome.[2]

Nerva died in January AD 98, having been emperor for only about fifteen months.[3] Trajan was still campaigning on the German front when the news of the Emperor's passing reached him in Lower Germany. The news of Nerva's death was delivered by Trajan's ward, the future emperor Hadrian. Rather than rushing back to Rome, the new emperor remained on the frontier for some time, finalising affairs in Germany, before engaging in a tour of the Danubian frontier and eventually returning to Rome in September or October of the following year.[4]

Trajan's tour of the Danube was not simply a matter of the new emperor inspecting the region. He clearly had plans to finish what Domitian had started because:

> He took into account their past deeds and was grieved at the amount of money they were receiving annually, and he also observed that their power and pride were increasing.
>
> Dio, LXVIII, 6.1.

The new emperor's tour was used to begin the preparations for a war against the Dacians. Trajan's Dacian wars were incredibly hard-fought but finally brought matters with the Dacians to an end, and led to the last Roman annexation of new territory. By the end of Trajan's reign the Empire had reached the greatest extent it ever would.

The evidence for Trajan's Dacian wars is significantly better than the evidence for much of the preceding campaigns. But although Trajan himself wrote on account of the Dacian wars, unfortunately all but five words of that account are lost to us and what remains translates as: 'First we went to Aizi then we went to Berzobis', providing us with at least an understanding of the first incursion into Dacian territory by this emperor, but not much else. Additionally, there is not much by the way of literary source material available for these wars, the best by far being that of Cassius Dio, but even this is critically limited. However, what we do possess is a unique record in the form of Trajan's Column. It presents an account of the Dacian wars in picture form, presented over a 220m-long spiral freize wrapped around a column placed in the heart of Rome in Trajan's Forum to commemorate the victory he had achieved. There are clear biases associated with the representations on the Column, but the underlying course of the wars can be determined by close examination of the images presented.

Trajan's Column

Trajan's Column is a beautifully-worked piece of art and architecture that has been the subject of significant debate by modern scholars. Its construction makes it clear that it was manufactured by professional artists who very likely had never been in Dacia or seen a Dacian. The depictions of individual Dacian soldiers or Roman legionaries cannot be considered as accurate representations of what they looked like on the battlefield – rather, they illustrate a conventionalized interpretation of their appearance. The purpose of the Column was clearly to impress upon the citizenry and visitors to Rome the glory of Trajan's victories rather than provide an exact depiction of the forces involved. The representations therefore reflect what a Roman citizen would have expected a Dacian or a Roman legionary to look like. As such, the spiral frieze on the Column cannot be used for evidence of Dacian armour or weapons, and can only be used as evidence for the latest, most up-to-date Roman legionary equipment, as that is all that is depicted. The monument at Adamklissi highlights this well, as the depictions on that, although less finely crafted, illustrate Roman soldiers in a variety of different equipment to that depicted on Trajan's Column.

The Adamklissi Monument was built by soldiers who actually took part in the war and as a result present a far more realistic indication of Roman military equipment during this period. It illustrates clearly that not every legionary was equipped with the latest type of armour, the *lorica segmentata*: rather the soldiers depicted on the monument wear older *lorica hamata* (chain mail) and *lorica squamata* (scale) armours.[5] Additionally, Trajan's Column depicts none of the changes to Roman armour introduced in order to protect the legionaries more effectively against Dacian weapons. Conversely, the Adamklissi Monument depicts both the use of the *manica* worn on the legionary's sword arm and the addition of cross-bracing on the helmet.

The appearance of the Column today is very different to how it would have looked to Romans at the time of its construction. In its original form it would have been completely painted and many of the weapons and standards carried by the legionaries depicted on it were made from metal and inserted into holes in the marble. These details are now all missing as they were removed and melted down centuries ago. What remains is the sculptured frieze, although some damage and degradation has occurred over the years including at least one cannonball hole and decay due to acid rain as the Column is exposed to the elements. However, there are three Napoleonic-era casts of the column that are available for viewing which were made before much of the environmental damage had occurred. These are also particularly helpful as, depending on how they are displayed, they make a close examination of the individual scenes far easier than on the original.

Validity of the depictions?

Arguments have raged as to whether or not the depictions on Trajan's Column have any validity as historical evidence, ranging from authors who suggest that actual geographical locations can be determined through a close examination of the Column to others who suggest that it is nothing more than a piece of imperial propaganda with no value as evidence for the Dacian wars at all. As has already been said, it must be accepted that the Column presents a conventionalized depiction of Romans and Dacians alike, and that with only a few distinct exceptions, trying to determine the exact geographical location illustrated is pointless. However, a close examination of the scenes does provide the most complete narrative of the Dacian wars we currently have available.

Why did Trajan Attack the Dacians?

There have been a number of suggestions why Trajan attacked the Dacians. The three reasons most frequently given by modern authors are the Emperor's desire or need for money, a need for glory to help legitimize his reign and the threat posed by the Dacians to the security of the Empire's Danubian frontier.[6] Dacia was known to be extremely wealthy, with a number of very profitable goldmines that remain some of the biggest mines in the region even today. The Dacian wealth in precious metals is extremely clear, with the Romans exporting 165,500kg of gold and twice that amount of silver after the end of the Dacian wars. In addition to this Dacia was wealthy in salt, stone, iron and timber, making it an extremely attractive target for the Romans and clearly a province that could support a garrison. Glory was always a concern for Roman emperors, particularly for those who had very little military experience prior to becoming emperor such as Claudius, Nero and Domitian, who all tried to legitimize their reign through military action. Trajan, coming from a rather obscure but militarily active background, might have seen an active and successful return to the annexationist policies of Augustus and before him the Republic as a way to strengthen his position, but in reality he had little need to force an issue unnecessarily as his acceptance by the army was beyond doubt. Strobel estimated that the population of pre-annexation Dacia could have been in the vicinity of 1,000,000 people: based on a likely percentage of military-aged males in similar communities this suggests that there may have been between 200,000 and 250,0000 warriors available.[7] These would have been supplemented by the allies Dacia was able to call upon, illustrating that the Dacian monarch had access to a force large enough to make the invasion of neighbouring Roman provinces possible.

Some modern authors believe that the Romans only viewed the Dacians as a local threat,[8] but this is just too simplistic an assessment. As discussed in the previous chapter, any sign of Roman weakness on this frontier could lead to multiple incursions by multiple enemies, something that the Roman army with its limited manpower could not have coped with easily or for long. Trajan, having witnessed the events of Domitian's reign and the response, had good reason to attack the Dacians for all of the above reasons. United under Decebalus, the Dacians were clearly a threat to the security of the Danubian frontier, their conquest would win a great deal of wealth and there can be no doubt that a successful conquest of a people which had been an enemy of Rome since the time of Caesar would inevitably be glorious.

Trajan's Preparations on the Danubian Frontier

Trajan decided that upon becoming emperor, rather than returning directly to Rome, his position was secure enough and the threat posed by the Dacians serious enough to warrant his immediate attention. So he travelled to the Danubian provinces and spent the winter of AD 98 and all of AD 99 in Moesia, securing the frontier. He did this because he understood the threat posed by Decebalus and the Dacians and that Domitian's treaty had not settled it. His actions on the Danube demonstrate the importance he gave to securing the defences against the Dacians. In addition to ensuring that the discipline of the local troops was given special attention, Trajan had fortresses built on the left bank of the Danube across from Northern Pannonia, adding to those that had been built by Lentulus after the Dacian raids of 10 BC.[9] These could be used as waypoints for an invading force, providing them with forward bases, and they also functioned the way Lentulus's fortresses had, acting as an exclusion zone for native settlements, creating a buffer zone between Roman territory and the Dacians. Trajan also had the wooden auxiliary fortresses along the Danube rebuilt in stone and engaged in a building programme which ensured sufficient accommodation was available for an invasion force.[10] There can be no doubt that Trajan took the issue of Dacia very seriously.

He orchestrated the reconstruction of the Djerdap towpath that had been originally built under Domitian and also had a canal dug alongside the most hazardous parts of the Danube, allowing river traffic to bypass the hazardous rapids.[11] The 3km stretch that was bypassed demonstrates the importance of the construction. The river that ran alongside the canal flowed at approximately 18km per hour through a narrow channel containing ridges and rocks that formed an unnavigable set of rapids in at least two places. The canal allowed the Roman vessels to be moved off the river itself into the safe waters of the canal where oxen would be harnessed to the bows of the vessels which would then be towed up the canal until they could rejoin the river at a safer point.

This construction was important as it ensured that Roman forces based along this frontier, and any future invasion force, possessed secure logistics which were essential to maintaining an army in the region. Additionally, making navigation of the Danube safer ensured that the Danubian fleets that had been established by Vespasian and based nearby would be able to patrol the frontier more effectively, and when necessary transport troops to areas of conflict far more rapidly than if they had to march there. Trajan's Column illustrates the Emperor, accompanied by a relief force, sailing down the Danube to relieve the besieged Roman fortress after the end of the first campaign of the first war which has been referred to as the Moesian counter-attack, demonstrating the utility of the canals and towpaths built by the Romans.[12]

Trajan also had a walkway carved into the side of a cliff in order to provide troops with safe access into enemy territory. This was constructed by excavating a small path out of the rock face, adding significant bracing and building a wider wooden walkway. These preparations to secure the frontier would have been extremely expensive, both in terms of manpower and money which demonstrates the importance Trajan placed on the security of the Danubian frontier.

Domitian had apparently already begun bringing more troops into Moesia Superior and Inferior to reinforce the frontiers against the Dacians. However, Trajan further increased the number of auxiliaries based in Moesia Superior by either four or five cohorts in preparation for the first Dacian war,[13] but evidence indicates that either after the first campaign or the first war Trajan realized that he still did not have sufficient troops at his disposal and moved a further six cohorts into the province. After the completion of the first campaign in AD 101 he brought two new auxiliary units into Moesia Inferior in order to shore up the defences in this region also. This shows Trajan's foresight as in the winter of AD 101 to 102 the troops in Moesia Inferior were attacked by Dacian forces from across the Danube.

Decebalus

Decebalus was a charismatic military commander respected by his people and his enemies as an excellent leader, strategist and tactician.[14] Trajan's comprehensive preparations indicate that he took Decebalus's ability very seriously. Decebalus was considered an excellent military commander by his own people, as is demonstrated by the fact that Duras, the previous king, abdicated in his favour because he was deemed to be the better military leader. It is clear from the accounts that Decebalus quickly earned for himself a reputation as an excellent military commander beyond his own people, which he cemented by defeating the Roman forces of Fuscus sent against him in AD 86. The clever ambush that led to his victory against Fuscus and to the loss of an entire Roman legion demonstrates the validity of his reputation. Decebalus had a very good understanding of his enemy and the capabilities of his own forces. He was well aware that defeating a Roman invasion was likely to be extremely difficult, and it appears that he actively pursued the creation of an anti-Roman alliance. The sources hint at the possibility that Decebalus may have been trying to convince the Parthians to participate in the war against Rome, although this never happened. He also approached the Germans and Sarmatians, and that he achieved some success in his endeavour is clear, with depictions of both Germans and Sarmatians fighting with the Dacians against the Romans on both Trajan's Column and the crenallations of the Adamklissi Monument which show the defeated forces and their allies.

Trajan's First Campaign, AD 101

Trajan left for Dacia on 25 March, surrendering an ordinary consulship in order to begin his first war against the Dacians. The fact that he surrendered a consulship he had already begun might suggest that something occurred on the frontier involving the Dacians that required an immediate response, but if so, we don't know what it was. There is a continuing discussion regarding the course of the first and second Dacian wars, with a recent publication suggesting an alternate route that may have been taken by Trajan's forces in their first campaign.[15] Considering the current state of research, it is almost impossible to determine with any certainty which of the two predominant theories regarding the Roman advance into Dacia is more likely correct. Both have commendable elements and demonstrate that Trajan's Dacian war was not as simplistic as might otherwise have been believed.

The Romans did not make it far into Dacia before the end of the campaigning season. It seems evident that Decebalus's strategy for defeating the Romans rested on keeping them away from the Dacian fortifications. The longer Decebalus kept the Romans from inflicting any tangible damage, the longer he would have to try to organize an anti-Roman coalition. It would have been relatively clear to Decebalus that the Roman advance would take time, especially taking into account that he had an understanding of the manner in which the legions operated, stopping every night to construct a marching camp.

Decebalus had the Dacians abandon the low-lying territories in Dacia.[16] By doing so before the Roman forces approached, Decebalus was able to concentrate his forces in the Oraştie mountains, as a result he was able to fully man the fortress network in the region. Decebalus understood the strengths and weaknesses of the Dacians and the Romans. Taking these into account, he was unwilling to face the Roman legions on the flat arable land of the valleys. To do so would have allowed the Romans to make use of their heavily-armoured legionaries on terrain most suitable for the use of the close-order tactics which they were famous for. Instead the Dacians withdrew into the mountains, in an effort to draw the legionaries into terrain that was less suitable to them, minimizing their strengths. This strategy is clearly illustrated on the Column, which shows the Roman forces marching through the lowland regions unopposed.[17] The focus of the depictions here are the Roman legionaries involved in the day-to-day tasks whilst on campaign, like constructing their marching camps. The first evidence of a Dacian warrior doesn't occur until Scene XVIII on the Column and this Dacian is on his own. It can be presumed that he had been sent to monitor the Roman advance. In the scene he is dragged before the emperor by a Roman auxiliary for questioning.

The *Epitome* of Dio tells us that as Trajan neared Tapae, which is where the Dacians had set up their camp, he was approached by a messenger bearing a mushroom which had writing on it in Latin advising him to turn around and keep the peace. Of course the Emperor had no intention of leaving Dacia without a victory and continued his advance. The first military contact between the Dacian forces and the Romans occurred at Tapae, where the Dacians tried to make use of the close and heavily-forested terrain in an attempt to defeat the Roman forces sent against them as they had Domitian's first army at the same place. Trajan's Column provides very interesting evidence for the tactics employed by both forces during this battle.

A close examination of the relevant scenes on the Column indicates that the Romans did not use the legionaries as their primary assault force to defeat the Dacians at Tapae.[18] Rather the depictions seem to indicate that the legionaries were held back, possibly in reserve, and that it was the auxiliaries who made contact with the Dacians at Tapae and defeated them. Scene XXIV on the Column shows Trajan in the centre of the scene on an elevated dais. He is facing the viewer to his right, facing left are legionaries in front of the Emperor and to his left are the auxiliary forces, both cavalry and infantry: two of the auxiliaries offer Trajan the severed heads of Dacian warriors. The following scene shows more Roman auxiliaries wearing mail armour directly engaged with Dacian warriors, and additionally German native troops fighting with the Romans are shown in the front line swinging clubs at Dacians. The Dacians are depicted streaming out of the forests. Most of the Dacians shown are the *comati*, the long-haired ones, who belonged to the lower class, but there are a few *pilleati*, cap-wearing nobility, and one of these located amongst the trees is Decebalus. This scene also shows several Dacians lying dead at the feet of the advancing Roman auxiliaries and one, clearly wounded, being carried away from the battle by his comrades. Another particularly interesting feature in this scene is the depiction of the god Jupiter located above the battle apparently surrounded by draped material, his right arm is drawn back, the weapon is missing but would presumably have been a lightning bolt. He is targeting the Dacians below and is clearly supporting the Roman forces in their first battle against the barbarians.

For the Romans, the use of their auxiliary forces to at least spearhead the attack made perfect sense considering the nature of the terrain which would likely have made the use of the legionaries problematic. The auxiliaries were more lightly armed and armoured than the legionaries and as a result probably far more suited to fighting in this type of terrain. Additionally, the auxiliaries would have been more able to fight in open formations necessary in this type of terrain and less reliant on close formations for success. The Dacian forces are shown in a very conventionalized fashion with no signs of armour other than the oval shield. Again almost all the weapons are missing from the Dacians' hands with only an arrow visible in the hands of one of the figures, and another depicted holding a bow. The majority of the Dacians are depicted as if engaged in an overhead swing, most likely with a *falx*. Dio tells us that although the Romans won the battle at Tapae and many Dacians were killed, many Roman troops were wounded.[19] The battle led to so many injuries on the Roman side that Dio tells us that the Romans ran out of bandages, and that Trajan tore up his own cloak in order to provide more.[20]

After the battle of Tapae Trajan continued into the Oraștie mountains. Dio tells us that the Emperor captured some of the fortified settlements in the mountains, and the Column shows Roman troops burning settlements in the mountains and the Emperor standing before an imposing Dacian fortification, examining the formidable defences.[21] This fortress has been identified as possibly being Costeşti. The depiction of Costeşti on the Column is particularly interesting for a number of reasons, the first being that it is depicted as possessing a number of features designed to prevent assault, including spiked pits. There are also a number of additional features present at Costeşti clearly intended to provide the Dacian warriors with the supplies necessary to with stand a prolonged siege, such as the water towers depicted.[22]

The first campaign ended with Dacian envoys sent to the Emperor to try and negotiate a settlement, as described in Dio's account, apparently Decebalus would not meet either Trajan or his generals in person and probably as a result of this the talks broke down. Trajan's first campaign against the Dacians ended with the onset of winter which prevented the Romans continuing their advance and bringing the campaign to a decisive end.

The Moesian counter-attack

In the winter after the end of the first campaign, when the Romans had retired to their winter camps, a Dacian force crossed the Danube and attacked the Roman fort in the province of Moesia. There is some debate concerning the timing of this event, with one well-known author arguing that because the river depicted is not frozen and the Dacian king is not present in any of these scenes, that it occurred at the same time as Trajan's first campaign. He suggests that the counter-attack was a clever Dacian strategy intended to end the Roman advance into the Carpathians by attacking positions in their rear and forcing Trajan to turn his forces around to defend Roman territory. Although this is an interesting theory, the fact the river isn't frozen does not suggest that the attack depicted did not occur during the winter, as the river didn't always freeze and would not freeze early in the season anyway. Although the fact that Decebalus isn't present suggests that he was busy elsewhere, this did not have to be actively fighting Romans as suggested by Daicoviciu, rather it is just as likely that he was busy trying to organize an anti-Roman alliance.[23] Because it seems unlikely that the Dacian forces would be able to move from the Oraștie mountains past the attacking Romans in order to launch an attack in Moesia, and because of the advantages in attacking the Romans when dispersed in their winter quarters, it seems more likely that the attack did take place in the winter after the first campaign. Additionally, the fact that the Romans are shown arriving by boat as opposed to crossing the Danube lends additional weight to the argument that this occurred after the Romans gone into winter quarters and demonstrates the value of the towpaths that made river transport possible.

The crossing itself is depicted on Trajan's Column in Scenes XXXI – XLI. It is portrayed in a chaotic scene, where mounted Dacians are shown in the water and some Dacian warriors being pulled from the turbulent waters by others. In the background a troop of heavily-armoured Sarmatian horsemen support the Dacian attack on the Roman fort. The Sarmatian Roxolani, who dwelt to the east of the Carpathians, were a significant nuisance to the Romans both before and after the Dacian annexation. These horsemen are the only heavily-armoured enemy of the Roman forces depicted on the Column. Trajan's conquest of Dacia was not the first time the Roxolani had come to the attention of Rome. The Roxolani were already allied to the Dacians during the reign of Burebista, during Nero's reign they are also mentioned, still as allies of the Dacians, and during Domitian's reign they participated in at least two attacks on Roman territory, resulting in the death of the Roman governor of Moesia, Fronteius Agrippa. These Sarmatians remained allies of the Dacians throughout the entire first Trajanic war, but there is some uncertainty regarding their allegiance during the second war as they might have been paid off by the Romans before its outbreak.

A perplexing element of the Column's depiction of the Roxolani is the fact that they are pictured using bows, not melee weapons. The use of a bow whilst wearing heavy armour seems counter-intuitive as ranged attackers would likely benefit more from speed than additional protection. In this case, because the horses too are heavily armoured, the depiction of a ranged weapon is even more perplexing. It seems far more likely that the Roxolani, who were known to have fought with a long spear, used that weapon during this war and that the depiction of the bow is most likely a mistake made by the artists responsible for the carving of the Column who are unlikely to have ever seen an actual Sarmatian. Dacians were known to use bows from horseback and this depiction might therefore be the result of a conflation of the two ideas.

This sequence of scenes illustrates a number of interesting features about the Dacian army. Even by the fifth century AD barbarian attacks against Roman fortifications were likely to fail, and in fact in the majority of cases these forces could not even manage to get past the outermost defensive lines, let alone reach the walls of the Roman fortifications. The depictions on the Column, however, make it clear that the Dacians understood Roman fortifications and how to breach them. Scene XXXII clearly shows the Dacians, having already bypassed the outer defences, attacking the walls of the fortress. Dacian archers shoot at the Roman auxiliaries trying to defend the walls, forcing them to keep their heads down, whilst another element of the Dacian forces use a battering ram in an attempt to gain entry into the fortress. The fact that they were able to bypass the outer fortifications and attack the walls with siege equipment is an indication of the Dacians' expertise, possibly a result of the training they had received from the Roman experts supplied by Domitian or the deserters recruited by Decebalus.

The importance of Decebalus's counter-attack is clearly evident by the Roman response to it, which is also depicted on the Column. The Roman reinforcements are shown rushing to the assistance of the besieged fortress in small oared vessels. The reliefs show unarmoured legionaries packed aboard the vessels, with auxiliaries and horses also. These troops are led by Trajan himself and after they are shown disembarking auxiliaries and cavalry, again led by the Emperor, chase and engage the heavily-armoured Sarmatians shown assisting the Dacians in the assault on the Moesian fortress. The next scene illustrates a night battle where the Dacians appear to have been encircled by Roman auxiliary cavalry on one side and auxiliary infantry supported by club-wielding German allies on the other.[24] Trajan is shown meeting with a small group of Dacian nobility in a newly-built fortress or fortified camp, whilst the combat scenes continue with images of wounded Romans, both legionaries and auxiliaries, being treated by military doctors, and for the first time on the Column the legionaries are depicted involved in the fighting against the Dacians. After the final combat sequence of the counter-attack, the Dacians flee into the forests to escape the Romans. The fact that Trajan himself led the reinforcements and sailed down the Danube in order to relieve the Moesian fort signifies how serious the threat from this counter-attack actually was.

Of particular interest in Trajan's Dacian wars is the use of fortifications by the Dacian forces, including an earthen embankment where the terrain narrowed, making the Roman advance significantly more difficult than it might otherwise have been. Some archaeological evidence demonstrates the use of this sort of defensive work on the Iron Gates, which is believed by some to have been the pass utilized by Trajan to make his way to Sarmizegetusa Regia. Other authors, notably Stefan, believe that the Trajan made his way there through the region roughly analogous with modern-day Deva.

As has already been mentioned, after Burebista's creation of a unified Dacian state the number of fortifications built under the authority of the Dacian king increased substantially.[25] Decebalus was determined to make the best possible use of these fortifications during the Roman invasion. Not many are depicted on the Column during Trajan's first campaign, illustrating the fact the Romans did not manage to break into the Dacian heartland proper during this campaign. However, the number of fortresses depicted and attacked by the Romans on the Column increases as the illustration of Trajan's wars continues.

The primary evidence of the Dacian fortifications is of course their archaeological remains. Excavations therefore provide a lot of information about the size, placement and complexity of Dacian fortresses. Not all Dacian fortresses were permanently inhabited, although some possessed a permanent garrison made up of the Dacian nobility and their followers. The ordinary Dacian peasant lived in the fertile valleys, and would have been moved to the forts in wartime, thus bolstering the number of men available to their king. The archaeology also provides evidence for features such as water reservoirs and grain stores, making these highly sophisticated structures, in some cases capable of holding out against a besieging force for a protracted period of time, which is probably why there is no mention of the use of circumvallation and trying to starve the Dacians out. The Column clearly shows that the Romans took direct action against these very well-defended sites and assaulted the walls. There can be little doubt that this would likely cost more Roman lives in the short term, but trying to starve the well-supplied Dacians out might have done the same in the longer term. The Orastie mountains are no place to be without adequate shelter in the winter.

Unfortunately, the archaeology does not provide evidence of what, if any, defensive obstacles the Dacians had placed beyond the walls, but there are several depictions on Trajan's Column that provide some evidence for more complex defences that would not necessarily be readily identifiable in the archaeological record. A number of interesting defensive devices used by the Dacians to defend their fortifications are depicted on the Column including three-wheeled carts that appear to have spikes mounted on the front, which are pointing directly down a slope away from the fortification.[26] Their identity has been the subject of debate, but it seems likely that these were somehow related to the wagons described by Arrian when discussing the encounter between Philip II and the Getae.[27] The Getae unsuccessfully attempted to halt the advance of the Macedonian forces coming up a mountain after them but releasing weighted wagons which rolled down the slope at the Macedonians, the intention most likely being to disrupt the Macedonian formation, with the hope that some of them would be injured if not killed. The tactic was most likely based on the idea that a disrupted formation would be easier to attack, and in this instance had the wagons proved successful it is likely that the Getae would have followed up with a direct assault. However, in this case the Macedonian troops were so well trained that when they were given the order, those that could move to the sides of the path out of the way of the hurtling wagons and those that could not remove themselves from the wagons' path fell to the ground and hid under their shields for protection, allowing the wagons to pass over the top of them.

It seems likely that these wagons which had been used by the Getae, are related to the three-wheeled and weighted devices that appear that appear on the Column in front of a Dacian fortress awaiting use.[28] It is therefore probable that the Romans also had to face an attack similar to the one faced by Philip's Macedonians. The Romans were, of course, the equal of the Macedonians in training, suggesting that they reacted in a very similar manner and the wagons proved largely ineffective. Mantraps that resembling spiked pits are also depicted on the Column in front of the fortress which has been claimed to be Costesti. The tactic of slowing an enemy advance on fortresses using such obstacles was one regularly practised by the Romans, giving them extra time to damage the assaulting forces with missiles. It is likely the Dacians had adopted this tactic from the Roman engineers or deserters they had access to, if they weren't doing this before.

The second campaign

The Roman goal for the second campaign was to actually make it into the Dacian fortress network in the Orăştie mountains which they had only just managed to reach at the end of the first campaign. The Column illustrates the second campaign in a fairly short sequence, beginning with the Roman forces again crossing a pontoon bridge into Dacia. Trajan is shown in Dacia meeting with his troops and making the traditional sacrifices before the start of the campaign proper.[29] The Roman legionaries, working in armour, are then shown felling trees and constructing a road through the forested mountains of Dacia, their helmets and shields piled nearby, ready in case of ambush. These works are vital as in time they provided the troops access to the fortified Dacian settlements and fortresses in the mountains. Interestingly, in the following scene, where an assault on a fortified settlement is depicted, it isn't the legionaries that carry out the attack but again the Roman auxiliaries, who are shown torching a fortified settlement, while in the background the Dacians are escaping into the mountains.[30]

The next major engagement depicted again shows native auxiliaries, this time unarmoured Moorish cavalry, directly engaged with the Dacians whilst Trajan, at the head of the legions, is at the rear of the scene watching the battle unfold.[31] The horizontal spilt in the scene suggests two simultaneous engagements, both involving the Moorish cavalry, one higher up in the mountains than the other. The Moorish cavalry are clearly winning, as the Dacians are depicted escaping into the ubiquitous forests.

The Roman forces are shown fortifying their positions and mounting their artillery in the newly-constructed fortifications. The artillery depicted is the *ballista*, a torsion-powered bolt-thrower. These were not only used by the Romans to help defend their fortifications but are also depicted being used as field artillery, *carroballistae*, mounted on two-wheeled wagons pulled by horses or mules. Against most foes the use of these by the Romans would be a demonstration of their technological superiority, but this was not the case with the Dacians, who are also pictured using the exact same weapon in this campaign. The Dacian *ballista* is placed behind a palisade and is being used by bearded Dacians to defend the walls of one of their fortifications from the advancing Romans.[32]

The depictions of the second campaign continue with three more engagements. The first, led by Roman auxiliaries, German allies and Syrian archers, appears to have begun in the Orăştie mountains but ends in one of the numerous Dacian fortified settlements in the region after the Dacians apparently flee to the fort in an attempt to survive the Roman onslaught. The scene immediately following this battle shows a different Dacian fortress, evident by the different type of wall shown. This is the first time that the Roman legionaries are shown fighting in Dacia. They use the *testudo*, or tortoise, formation to assault the fortress, illustrating the strength of the legionary forces who are capable of attacking and overcoming the Dacian walls. The final combat scene of the first war follows, as under the emperor's supervision the Roman forces including slingers, German native allies, auxiliaries and legionaries, fight a force of Dacian warriors in front of another fortress. Clearly by the end of the first war the Romans had broken into the Dacian heartland and the scenes of Romans attacking fortresses and fortified settlements illustrate this. Trajan was able to recapture the Roman military standards that had been lost by Fuscus during Domitian's reign.[33] The first war ends with the victorious Trajan seated on a podium accepting the supplications of a group of Dacian nobles. The Column's depiction of the first war ends with the depiction of personified Victory inscribing a shield flanked by trophies made up of the arms and armour of the defeated Dacian and Sarmatian enemies.

The first war ended with the Dacian surrender when the Romans managed to reach their capital of Sarmizegetusa Regia. Trajan accepted the surrender, and even allowed Decebalus to remain king. The Dacians were to become a client kingdom required to support the Romans whenever asked. This created a buffer zone between the Roman frontier and the barbarian peoples even further north. Decebalus found himself in a situation where he was forced to agree to whatever terms the Emperor decided. This arrangement differed somewhat from the agreement he had reached with Domitian, but not by very much. Dio preserves the terms of the peace agreement reached.[34] The Dacians were required to surrender their arms, siege weapons and the technicians capable of manufacturing them. Decebalus was also required to surrender to Rome all deserters that had taken up the Dacian cause, he was to demolish his fortresses and evacuate land captured by Rome. The Dacians were not to shelter any Roman deserters nor were they allowed to employ any Roman soldiers. These terms are particularly interesting as they suggest that although Dacia was to become a client kingdom and buffer zone, Trajan was disarming Decebalus and destroying his fortifications, making Dacia's effectiveness as a buffer zone limited to say the least.

Although the way the first war was brought to an end makes it clear that Trajan's intention was not necessarily to annex Dacia from the start, otherwise he would have pushed on to achieve that goal and certainly would not have celebrated a victory over the Dacians until he had. The fact that he imposed quite harsh terms that saw the Dacians disarmed suggests that the Emperor always intended on finishing the conquest, either because he thought that the Dacians would make untrustworthy allies or alternatively it is also possible that the Roman forces were stretched during the first war and needed some time to regroup in preparation for a final push against their hardy and troublesome foe. Either way, Dio suggests that Decebalus was himself trying to buy time to regroup and never had any intention of abiding by the agreement with Trajan.[35] Decebalus sent envoys to the Senate which ratified Trajan's peace treaty with the Dacians. Trajan was awarded the title *Dacicus* and celebrated a hard-earned triumph.

Throughout the first war as a whole, it is interesting to note the relative success of Decebalus's strategy. He was able to keep the Romans away from the Dacian heartland during the first campaign, and he managed to significantly reduce the involvement of the legionaries for much of the first war through clever terrain choices. The legionaries are depicted on the column as engaged in building works, clearing forests and constructing roads, whereas the auxiliaries are shown patrolling, assaulting Dacian settlements and fighting in the heavily-wooded regions such as Tapae. In the end Decebalus's strategy possibly slowed the Roman advance but Rome's resources and manpower made their arrival in the Dacian heartland inevitable. Had he managed to create an anti-Roman alliance, or if he could have stirred up additional trouble for the Romans along the frontier, things might have been even more difficult still for them.

The Second Dacian War

The second Dacian war seems to have been a much less complicated affair for the Romans, though not necessarily much easier. Trajan had breached the heartland of Dacia at the end of the first war, many of their fortresses had been destroyed or badly damaged and even if Decebalus was rebuilding them, the period between the two wars was quite short and it seems highly unlikely that the Dacian king would have had the resources let alone the time to fully rebuild what had been damaged. Additionally, many amongst the highest-ranking Dacian nobility had lost the will to continue fighting against Rome and likely many decided to take the route of profitability over nationality and joined the Roman side in the coming conflict. The Romans were now well aware of both Decebalus's tactics and the locations of the important Dacian fortresses which formed the core of his ability to resist.

The second war, which began in 106 AD, was to see the Dacians finally conquered and Dacia become a province within the Roman Empire. Cassius Dio provides us with clear grounds for the beginning of the second war: he claims that Decebalus was being unfaithful to the terms of the peace treaty agreed to at the end of the first war, particularly in relation to the tearing down of forts, the stockpiling of weapons and the return of Roman deserters.[36] Decebalus went so far as to capture a part of the territory belonging to the Iazyges, which would become an issue between Rome and this Sarmatian tribe later. These breaches of the peace treaty provided Trajan the convenient excuse for once again making war on Decebalus this time with the clear intention of replacing the Dacian monarch with a Roman governor and annexing the mineral rich country of Dacia. It is possible that the treaty struck at the end of the first war was Trajan's way of pausing the war in order to be able to regroup and prepare for a final assault: either way Trajan was not going to allow the Dacian problem to continue. This war would see the Roman forces again reach the Dacian fortifications in the Oraştie mountains.

In the meantime, Decebalus continued to try and orchestrate an anti-Roman alliance with the peoples closest to him:

> Declaring that if they abandoned him they themselves would be imperilled, and that it was safer and easier for them, by fighting on his side before suffering any harm, to preserve their freedom.
>
> Dio. LXVIII.11.2.

Unfortunately for the Dacians, Decebalus was unable to create the sort of alliance he must have envisioned. In addition to his failure to convince nearby peoples to assist him, many Dacian nobles and their followers abandoned him. Now that almost everything was working against him, Decebalus realized that his chances of winning a war against Rome had almost vanished. He decided to set a rather deceitful plan into motion. Decebalus, knowing that during a time of war access to the commander was relatively easy as they needed to receive information from all available sources, sent some Roman deserters into Moesia in an attempt to have Trajan assassinated. The plan failed when one of the conspirators was arrested and gave away the plot after being examined under torture.

Decebalus next contacted one of Trajan's generals, Longinus, ostensibly to surrender under whatever terms were acceptable to the Romans. When Longinus came to meet the Dacian king he was taken prisoner. Decebalus questioned the Roman general about Trajan's plans, but Longinus refused to divulge any information. Having failed to get any information that might have helped him plan his defence, Decebalus, growing increasingly desperate, tried to bargain with Trajan for the general's life. He would return Longinus alive if Trajan returned all the territory that had been taken from the Dacians, left Dacia and paid a war indemnity to cover the costs Decebalus had sustained fighting the Romans. Trajan sent a calculatedly non-committal response that left Decebalus pondering the value of the Roman general. Longinus took matters into his own hands and with the help of a freedman acquired some poison. He then convinced Decebalus to send the freedman to Trajan in order to bargain for his release, which the Dacian king did. Once the freedman was safely away, Longinus took the poison and died. This angered Decebalus who offered to return the body of Longinus to Trajan with ten other captives if the freedman was sent back so the king could punish him, but the Emperor refused. Decebalus had lost most of his territory, many of the Dacian nobles that had supported him during the first war had abandoned his cause, his fortresses had been captured and his final appearance on Trajan's Column depicts him committing suicide before the Roman auxiliary cavalrymen pursuing him could capture him.[37] Decebalus's head was taken back to Trajan and was displayed during the emperor's triumph.

After the conclusion of the second war Trajan set about organizing the province. There has been some discussion about whether or not the Dacians were exterminated and replaced by colonists brought in from elsewhere in the Empire. This is based on one primary source suggesting that Trajan massacred the Dacians and the lack of Dacian names found in inscriptions after the Dacian defeat. However, archaeological evidence, including native pottery finds, clearly demonstrate a continuation of the Dacian people after the conclusion of the wars, and it is possible that a few native Dacians moved into the settlements where the inscriptions were found utilized Romanized names rather than Dacian ones. This said, a very large number of colonists were brought into Dacia after the annexation. Many of these were to be directly engaged in mining the wealth of the new province for the Romans.

As a result of the successful conquest of Dacia Trajan reorganized the province of Pannonia, splitting it into two, Pannonia Inferior and Pannonia Superior. The future emperor Hadrian was made the first governor of the former. The Sarmatian Iazyges petitioned Trajan to return to them the land in the Banat valley that the Dacians had taken from them and Rome had since taken from the Dacians. Trajan's refusal began a conflict with the Iazyges and Hadrian was forced to defend his province against the incursions of the Iazyges, a feat he was destined to repeat twenty years later in the first year of his reign as emperor.

Although in reality Trajan's victory over the Dacians was very hard won, the depictions of the war on Trajan's Column can easily be interpreted as depicting the Dacian wars as a relatively easy victory. The Dacian army that took the field against Trajan's forces was substantially more diverse, Romanized and professionally-equipped than is depicted either on the Column or in the literary account provided by Dio. Trajan managed to conquer this hardy and difficult foe, settling for all time Rome's Dacian problem. His victory was celebrated in Rome with a triumph and 123 days of games and celebrations.

Chapter 9

Hadrian

L ike Trajan before him, Hadrian was both a provincial and a military man who had risen through the ranks in the army. He had served in the first of Trajan's Dacian wars and commanded I *Minervia* in the second.[1] Hadrian was thus already extremely well versed in the circumstances on the Danube frontier when he became emperor.[2] Hadrian had clearly been one of Trajan's most trusted commanders: in fact his service in Dacia was so distinguished that he received two military awards from Trajan.[3] Soon afterwards he was appointed the first praetorian legate of Pannonia Inferior after Trajan split the province in two, giving him still more experience and a greater understanding about the nature of this frontier.[4] During his time there Hadrian had campaigned against the Sarmatian Iazyges who would again become a problem at the very beginning of his reign as *princeps*. The *Historia Augusta* indicates that his time in Pannonia was very successful and as a reward he was made consul by Trajan in AD 108.[5]

After he had completed his conquest of Dacia, Trajan continued his expansionist policies, conquering large tracts of the East whilst campaigning against the Armenians and the Parthians. Many believe that Trajan's continued expansion exceeded Rome's ability to garrison and govern such conquests effectively. Cassius Dio, whose account of Trajan's life and deeds was generally very positive, says that his real reason for attacking the Parthians and the Armenians was not the slight they had committed by not consulting the *princeps* about the appointment of a new Armenian king but rather his 'desire to win renown'.[6] With the accession of the new emperor, however, the recently reinvigorated policy of expansionism was brought to an end.

Hadrian began a policy of consolidation. He abandoned Trajan's eastern acquisitions almost immediately, a move that cannot have been popular with Romans unaccustomed to relinquishing conquered territory. In all likelihood Hadrian's actions were particularly unpopular with the legionaries who had fought for Trajan in the East and lost comrades there. Some sources suggest that as early as AD 116, less than a decade after Trajan's conquest, Hadrian seriously considered relinquishing Dacia. Although he decided against it, Hadrian did give up significant tracts of the territory Trajan had captured north of the Danube. He clearly feared that matters with the Dacians weren't permanently resolved and destroyed Trajan's

Danubian bridge that had been designed and built by the architect Apollodorus. Trajan had this immense bridge built so that he could move the Roman army into Dacian territory rapidly in response to any trouble. But Hadrian viewed the bridge very differently. He saw a risk that the Dacians might overwhelm the garrison guarding the bridge and use it to cross quickly into Roman territory.

Although Trajan had annexed Dacia, the importance of the Danube did not come to an end. After Trajan's death, Hadrian was forced to return to the Danube during his first year of his reign. It is likely that Pompeius Falco, the Governor of Moesia Inferior, informed Hadrian of the difficulties he faced in the region and the need to end the growing Sarmatian threat. Falco himself was already busily engaged in fighting the Sarmatian Roxolani and free Dacians (those Dacians living outside the Roman province of Dacia) at the beginning of Hadrian's reign.[7] The free Dacians were Dacian peoples living outside of the Roman province of Dacia. Similarly, the Governor of Pannonia was engaged in a conflict with the Sarmatian Iazyges and their allies the Quadi. Interestingly, this was far from the only threat the Empire faced at the time of Hadrian's accession, with Britain, Mauritania, Egypt and Judaea in revolt. Hadrian chose to deal with most of these problems through the appointment of qualified individuals. However, the issues on the Danube were too important to be entrusted to anyone else and Hadrian chose to deal with issues there himself. The new emperor travelled to the lower Danube as little as a month after his accession to the principiate. The fact that Hadrian chose to deal with issues on the Danube as rapidly as he did, combined with the fact that he went personally to the frontier in order to ensure a satisfactory solution, indicates the importance he placed on resolving these issues quickly.

Hadrian reorganized the personnel charged with protecting the frontier. He retained Pompeius Falco as the governor of Moesia Inferior as he was an experienced general, a former consul (in AD 108), and had been in charge of the region for at least two years prior to Hadrian's accession. Falco had direct military experience in the region as the commander of V *Macedonica* during Trajan's first Dacian war. Along with Quadratus Bassus, who was at the time the Governor of Dacia, Falco had been entrusted to lead the campaign against the free Dacians and the Roxolani. This was to claim the life of Bassus and it is conjectured that his replacement was Avidius Nigrinus, who we know from an undated dedication governed Dacia for a short period. Unfortunately, Nigrinus was not as lucky as Falco as he had fallen out of favour with Hadrian during Trajan's reign, and not long after the Emperor's arrival on the Danube he was replaced by Marcius Turbo, one of the new emperor's trusted friends.

This has been cited as one of the potential reasons for the supposed plot against Hadrian's life early in his reign, that saw four very important men, all of consular rank, put to death.[8] These purported conspirators had all been well-regarded by

Trajan and by the Senate. Although Hadrian rightly argued that he did not directly order their executions, the deaths of these four men besmirched Hadrian's reign to the extent that after his death it appears that the Senate did not wish to deify him and it was only thanks to his successor Antoninus Pius that he finally was. The four victims had all made it to the rank of consul, they had served as generals in Trajan's armies and, perhaps most tellingly, could all have been potential claimants to the principate.

Hadrian was confronted with a difficult situation; Trajan's conquests had created a bridgehead beyond the Danube that was potentially open to attack from three sides. Dacia became arguably the most exposed frontier of the Empire. After Trajan's death Hadrian actually considered relinquishing his conquests in Dacia and re-establishing the previous frontier along the Danube. Although in the end he did not do so, the fact that he considered this course of action illustrates the potential problems he foresaw along the Danube. As soon as he had become emperor Hadrian set about reorganizing the provinces.

The troubles faced by Hadrian came in the form of both of the Sarmatian tribes in the region, the Iazyges and the Roxolani, as well as the Germanic Quadi and Marcomanni. The German tribes are believed to have assisted the Iazyges who attacked the legionary forts at Campona, Vetus Salin and Intercisa between AD 117 and 119. Apparently Trajan had come to terms with the Iazyges and in return for their assistance against the Dacians had promised that after his conquest of Dacia was complete that he would return to them their homelands in the Banat Valley which been lost to the Dacians in an earlier conflict, but reneged on his agreement after the end of the war.[9] The Sarmatians were also angered by the fact that the Roman annexation of Dacia, and in particular the occupation of Oltenia, prevented them from undertaking their seasonal migrations along the Danube to meet up with the other Sarmatian tribe in the region, the Roxolani, who lived east of the Olt River in Wallachia. The reasons for German involvement at this time are not completely clear, but these tribes had faced Roman hostility when they refused to assist Domitian in his Dacian war, and were likely also concerned about Roman expansion and annexation so close to their own territory. Additionally there was a long-standing alliance between the Quadi and the Iazyges. The alliance between these two peoples appears to have been extremely close, with some shared communities. Hadrian managed the hostilities along the Danube with these German tribes but the fact that hostilities continued into the reigns of Antoninus Pius and Marcus Aurelius demonstrates that he was unable to end the troubles.[10]

The lack of Samian ware found in the Hungarian plains prior to the reign of Marcus Aurelius demonstrates that one of the Roman strategies employed against the Iazyges involved economic sanctions, by restricting free access to the Roman markets in the newly-constituted province.[11] It is only after many hard-fought battles during the Marcomannic wars that Rome came to terms with the Iazyges and lifted these restrictions.[12]

Roman troubles on the Danube were not confined to the issues with the Iazyges but also involved the other Sarmatian tribe north of the River, the Roxolani. After the conclusion of Trajan's wars, the Roxolani turned their attention from Moesia, which had been a frequent target of Sarmatian raids in the recent past, to the newly-established Roman province of Dacia. One suggestion is that the actions of the Roxolani can also be ascribed to the Roman domination of their homeland located in the region to the south of the Carpathians. There also appears to have been a complaint by the Roxolani king that the subsidies paid to his tribe had been reduced.[13]

Matters with the Roxolani were serious, resulting in the death of the Roman governor of Dacia who had been appointed by Trajan, Q. Julius Quadratus Bassus, in the spring of AD 118.[14] Bassus had been one of Trajan's most trusted generals, which was particularly important because of the problems Hadrian faced after the execution of four men of consular rank early in his reign. Bassus's death gave Hadrian an opportunity to demonstrate that it was not all of Trajan's generals that he had a problem with, and he did this by organizing for his body to be taken from Dacia all the way to his birthplace of Pergammon, accompanied by soldiers and greeted by local magistrates from all the cities along the way before having the body interred in a tomb built at public expense.

Hadrian seems to have been able to negotiate a peace with the Roxolani relatively quickly. The Sarmatian king was awarded Roman citizenship and took the new name P. Aelius Rasparaganus and, probably on the advice of Falco, Hadrian withdrew Roman forces from the Oltenian plains, Muntenia, South Moldavia and the south-eastern flank of the Carpathians giving up significant tracts of territory that had been won during Trajan's invasion.[15] It has also been suggested that during the course of the negotiations that the Roxolani king presented Hadrian with Borysthenes, a particularly well-bred horse that became Hadrian's favoured hunting mount.

Hadrian did withdraw forces from some of the most exposed regions around Dacia, in particular the garrisons that had been stationed on the plains to the east and west of the Dacian heartland in the Banat and Wallachia. These areas which had traditionally been controlled by Sarmatian tribes, the Banat by the Iazyges and Wallachia by the Roxolani. Hadrian's reign saw warfare in these regions between the Sarmatians and the Romans, although these threats were neutralized, the issues here demonstrated to Hadrian that there was no value in trying to retain control of these regions.

It appears that Hadrian remained on the Danube dealing with the Sarmatians through the spring and early summer of AD 118. It is possible that matters with the

Sarmatian Iazyges were not resolved by the time of his departure, and it appears likely that before he left, Hadrian became personally involved in the campaign against this tribe much as he had done as Governor of Pannonia Inferior twenty years earlier. By AD 120 Hadrian had made further changes to the organization of Dacia dividing the province into three separate commands: Dacia Inferior, located closest to the Danube, Dacia Superior, roughly covering the region of the Carpathian Mountains, and Dacia Porolissensis, which equated to the northern-most part of this province.[16] This arrangement would change again after 167 AD in order to accommodate Marcus Aurelius's campaigns.

Hadrian was responsible for a significant shift in the way the frontiers were managed, which also resulted in a dramatic change to the role of the Roman army during his reign. Hadrian's first six months in office illustrate continued issues along the Danube. He stabilized the Danubian frontier, and also spent a very large proportion of his time travelling the provinces and fortifying the most threatened borders.[17] Hadrian brought an end to expansion as the Roman frontier policy, focusing instead on using the army to defend the existing frontiers.

Chapter 10

The War of Many Nations

Matters on the Danube were still far from settled at the beginning of Marcus Aurelius's reign. Ironically, the emperor who would have been least likely to seek out military glory was forced to spend much of his principate engaged in conflict on the Danubian frontier, fighting a conglomeration of German peoples, primarily made up of the Marcomanni, the Quadi and numerous smaller tribes as well as the Sarmatian Iazyges. Again the factor that most contributed to the seriousness of the threat faced on the Danube was an uncommon degree of unity amongst Rome's enemies and the appearance of weakness in the frontier defences. The unity displayed here was reminiscent of that seen during the Pannonian rebellion which was defeated by Tiberius only after several years of hard fighting. The German peoples north of the Danube, although clearly working together to achieve their goals, displayed no evidence of centralization on the scale of the Dacians under Burebista or Decebalus. The Marcomannic War lasted from early in Marcus's reign until his death in AD 180, with only a brief break in the 170s. The *Historia Augusta* suggests that all of the peoples beyond the Rhine and the Danube conspired against Rome and that this war should rightfully be called a 'war of many nations'.[1]

There are a number of sources which mention the Marcomannic Wars and Marcus's campaigns along the Danube. However, as with so many of the campaigns in this region there is significantly more that we do not know than we can be certain about. The sources provide significantly more detail about the first war than the second. One of the primary problems with Marcus's campaigns is that they are incredibly difficult to accurately date, and debate continues about when these campaigns began, when the first war ended and when specifically-mentioned events occurred in the chronology of the wars as a whole. It is not possible to present all the arguments presented for the varying dates, and the most logical sequence of events has been followed here. Even the name Marcomannic Wars is the subject of debate, with some authors preferring other names such as the Danubian, Northern or Germanic Wars. The best sources for these wars are the *Historia Augusta*, which describes the life of Marcus Aurelius and provides some description of the wars fought in the north, and the abridgement of Cassius Dio which also provides significant details. Interestingly the *epitome* of Dio provides dates to accompany the events he describes, but it is clear that some of these dates are inaccurate and will be the subject of academic debate for many years to come.

Few details can be confidently asserted regarding the causes of these wars, but what seems unarguable is that pressure was being applied to some of the barbarian peoples situated closest to the Danube by the Goths, barbarians from further north. The reasons for this pressure are not clear, although suggestions have been made that land hunger, overpopulation and climate change were contributing factors in the Gothic push south. This pressure brought the Danubian tribes into conflict with Rome because they were ready to cross the frontier into Roman territory, even if that meant they had to force their way in because they could not get permission to enter from the emperors. It is really illuminating to realise that the Romans were seen as the lesser of two evils when the German and Sarmatian people had to choose whether to fight them or the Goths.

It is clear that both the author of the *Historia Augusta* and Dio believed that Marcus's actions here were designed to end with the annexation of two new regions, thereby adding to the Danubian frontier and securing this volatile area. Had Marcus managed to create these two new provinces of Marcomannia and Sarmatia, the geopolitical situation along the Danubian frontier would have been fundamentally changed.[2]

Direct Roman intervention in the middle Danube region had been going on for some time, with small units of soldiers being stationed amongst the barbarian tribes at the latest by the end of the reign of Antoninus Pius (AD 161), in an attempt to make certain that the less-than-reliable Germanic clients behaved themselves. Increasingly throughout Marcus's reign small detachments of troops are seen billeted in Roman towns also to help protect them against low-level threats.[3] Prior to the outbreak of the Marcomannic Wars cross-border trade between Rome and the peoples of the middle Danube was a mutually-beneficial arrangement that ensured continued and frequent contact. Peace in the region was largely the result of an obvious and significant Roman military presence. However, much of the garrison in or near this region had to be withdrawn by Marcus and his co-emperor Lucius in the early 160s AD for use against the Parthians when war broke out in the East. Even then, the forces Marcus was able to assemble still proved insufficient to bring the Eastern campaign to a successful conclusion, so in AD 165 two new legions were raised, the first for many years. The new legions were used to replace more seasoned troops on the Danubian frontier that were sent to the East, trying to ensure that the frontier didn't appear weakened to the barbarians north of the Danube. Matters became grimmer still when the troops returning from the East were afflicted by a plague.[4]

In AD 165–6 the situation on the Danube changed significantly and drew the Emperor's attention. A number of the German tribes north of the Danube had decided to settle within the Empire as a result of external pressure applied to Rome's German and Sarmatian neighbours located north of the Danube who were forced against the frontier by their more northerly Gothic neighbours. This pressure led to requests for admission into the Roman Empire and ultimately to demands for admission after they were refused. The Emperor's refusal to allow the Germans in was the cause of much of the trouble during Marcus Aurelius's reign. In addition to those wanting to settle in Roman territory because they were being pushed toward the frontier by the Goths, Dio tells us that others like the Marcomanni and the Victuali were throwing everything into confusion, suggesting that at least some of the Germans were engaged in opportunistic raiding and pillaging, contributing to the problems on the Danube.[5]

As a result, Rome although still involved in the Parthian war, was forced into a second war with the Marcomanni, the Victuali, the Quadi and numerous other tribes along the Danube. This war situated north of the Danube had been on the cards for some time, but active diplomacy had been used to stall its outbreak for as long as possible in order to give the co-emperors Marcus and Lucius an opportunity to bring the Parthian war to an end first. To make matters worse for Marcus at the same time as war broke out with the Danubian Germans and Sarmatians Rome was suffering from a very serious plague which had been brought back by troops returning from the East and would certainly have enhanced the terror felt by the Roman people.[6]

The *Historia Augusta* lists the number of peoples fighting against the Romans, going so far as to say that all the nations from the borders of Illyricum even into Gaul banded together against the Romans, and suggesting that rather than being just a Germanic war, it was in fact a war involving many more peoples.[7] Specifically mentioned as participants are the Marcomanni, the Varistae, the Hermunduri, the Quadi, the Suebians, the Sarmatians, the Lacringes, the Buri, the Victuali, the Osi, the Bessi, the Cobotes, the Roxolani, the Bastarnae, the Alani, the Peucini and the Costoboci. Even more are mentioned in other sources, including a number of smaller German tribes.

Although not armed with a unique weapon like the Dacians or as iron-rich, these other trans-Danubian peoples posed a significant threat to Roman frontier security as subsequent events illustrate. Archaeological examinations of various sites north of the Danube have demonstrated that the Quadi and Sarmatians had a very long alliance and often lived in close contact with each other, so much so that many sites in the frontier zone between these peoples show that the two peoples lived together in mixed communities,[8] leading to a degree of unity that made them difficult to defeat. The Quadi were known for their fierce warriors and substantial numbers and the Sarmatians were talented horsemen, capable of inflicting serious damage to Roman forces sent against them. The Marcomanni were arguably the most dangerous opponent to Rome throughout Marcus's reign. This explains the tendency to name these wars after them, rather than calling them the Danubian or Northern Wars which would be more accurate considering the enemies Rome faced. The Romans had encountered the Marcomanni before. Tiberius had fought against the Marcomannic King Maroboduus near the Elbe River, which is where the Marcomanni were still living early in the first century AD. But they and the Quadi had moved gradually southwards towards the Marus River, a tributary of the Danube, and settled in the regions opposite Pannonia near Carnuntum before the outbreak of this conflict.[9]

The First Marcomannic War

There is considerable debate about when the first war began. Many have dated its outbreak to either 169 or 170 AD, but by doing so they ignore the crossing of the Danube by the 6,000 barbarians mentioned in Dio's account.[10] He wrote than in AD 166 or 167 6,000 Langobardi and Obii crossed the Danube into Pannonia. These barbarians are not mentioned at all in the *Historia Augusta* as participating in these wars.[11] The Langobardi, or the Lombards as they were also known, were thought to live much further north than the Marcomanni at this time, making Dio's account somewhat problematic. Dio sees the crossing of the Danube by these tribes as the onset of the first Marcomannic War and provides sufficient detail that his account, although unconfirmed by the *Historia Augusta* should not be ignored. Dio tells us that this group of barbarians was defeated by Vindex and Candidus, both of whom were stationed in the region with a mixed force of infantry and cavalry.[12] Therefore, an earlier date of 167 AD for the outbreak of the war is more logical as it includes this major event which was clearly contributing factor to the start of these wars.

Following the invasion of the Langobardi and their allies, the legate of upper Pannonia, Bassus, led the peace negotiations between the Romans and the barbarians. Included in these negotiations were a number of tribes not mentioned as having participated in the invasion itself. Why would peoples not involved in the invasion have been forced to seek peace with Rome? The only logical conclusion is that several other peoples played a minor role at the very least in the invasion of Roman territory at this time, although they are not specifically mentioned as having done so in the sources. Bassus seemingly managed to negotiate suitable peace terms, but these were not to last for long, as it appears that either in the year AD 168 or 169 there must have been a number of crossings of the Danube by barbarian tribes. It was in response to the latest crossing that Marcus decided to assemble a force and respond in person to the barbarian threat. Together with his co-emperor Lucius Verus, he assembled a force with the intention of driving the barbarians out of Roman territory.[13] As they were about to leave Italy with their newly-assembled force, rumour of the advance had reached the barbarians and they though better of their plans, retreating back across the Danube.

The emperors were not deterred from going to the front themselves, although the sources suggest that Lucius was less than keen on leaving Rome, quite possibly because he had only just returned from fighting in the East. Both emperors advanced to Aquileia, The barbarians in the meantime put their own leaders to death in an effort to demonstrate to Rome that they had punished the individuals responsible for the incursion and that no further punishment was necessary, and they sent envoys to Marcus to sue for peace.[14] After concluding various peace agreements, Marcus and Lucius returned to Aquileia and set about organizing new defensive structures to protect, in particular, the roads into Italy and Rome, showing that Marcus knew matters were far from resolved and that Rome's most immediate weakness was the speed with which an invader could enter its territory.

However, while the emperors were in Aquileia, the plague became much worse in the region with the Roman commander Furius Victorinus and a very significant number of troops dying of it. The nature of the plague itself is a mystery, although it is known that it was brought back by Roman soldiers who had served in the East and was responsible for the deaths of many civilians and soldiers. What is uncertain, however is what this disease actually was, suggestions having included bubonic plague, smallpox or even typhus.[15] The fact that the plague was now prevalent in the vicinity of Aquileia saw the co-emperors decide to return to Rome in 169. Lucius Verus died on the journey, leaving Marcus the sole emperor. Marcus only mourned the loss of his son-in-law and co-emperor for five days before having to rush back to the Danubian theatre.

The resulting reduction in troop numbers in the region likely contributed to another crossing of the Danube by barbarian forces, which resulted in the first major counter-attack by the Romans. This first major engagement with the Danubian Germans was an odd affair, and resulted in a disastrous defeat for the Romans. The date of this engagement is very difficult to determine with some sources not even mentioning it all. Apparently Marcus had received a very strange portent whilst in Rome suggesting that if he made many sacrifices into the Danube including, very curiously, two lions, that the Romans would be successful in their endeavour against the trans-Danubian barbarians. Marcus apparently had these instructions carried out, but the two lions did not drown as was expected but rather swam across the Danube where they were promptly clubbed to death by the Germans on the other side. The offensive was no more successful than the sacrifice of the lions, the Romans being soundly defeated, some sources indicating that as many as 20,000 Roman troops were killed on the far side of the Danube. It seems most likely that this occurred in the time between Marcus's and Lucius's departure from Aquileia and Marcus's return to the front after mourning Lucius's passing, and it makes sense to assume that this defeat was the reason Marcus felt he had to hurry back to the frontier.

This must have been disastrous for Roman morale which would have already been suffering quite badly due to the effects of the plague, repeated Germanic incursions into Roman territory and now a significant defeat. Making matters even worse, the disaster encouraged other tribes along or near the Danube to also cross into Roman territory whilst the army was distracted and weakened. One major incursion saw Dacia invaded by Gothic peoples from the north.

Of course matters were compounded even further by the losses Rome had suffered both militarily against the Germans and as a result of the plague brought back from the East, which together had significantly weakened the Roman military forces. Extreme measures were needed in order to raise sufficient troops to be able to deal with the combined forces Rome faced. As a result the Emperor was forced to recruit from the most undesirable, and normally unimaginable, sources before he left for the frontier in October AD 169.[16] Only citizens could join the legions, although any freeborn man could join the auxiliaries. Freedmen could also join, although there seem to have been reservations about them, but slaves were strictly forbidden from joining the army. It was relatively common for slaves to illegally enlist in the army, most doing so to escape servitude, but they were punished if discovered.

Only in extreme circumstances were slaves accepted as volunteers in the Roman army. This was one of those occasions: Marcus permitted slaves and gladiators to enlist in the army to make up the much-needed numbers. These slaves were granted their freedom upon enrolment which would certainly have acted as a significant inducement to enlist.[17] Being an extremely rare expedient, this very clearly illustrates how bad a position the Empire found itself in and how desperately it needed to increase the available military manpower. By way of comparison, another occasion where the Romans allowed slaves to enlist in the army was immediately after the battle of Cannae during the Second Punic War which had resulted in immense losses, Polybius suggesting about 75,000 Romans and allies, although Livy suggests the more conservative figures of 45,000.[18] Whichever is correct, these figures illustrate the dire circumstances required before Rome considered allowing slaves to volunteer for military service, further demonstrating the severity of the situation Marcus was facing on the Danubian front. It would be wrong, however, to imagine that all Germans were somehow involved in this invasion of Roman territory. Many Germanic mercenaries were recruited by the Romans to serve as auxiliaries against their Quadi and Marcomanni brethren. Additionally, due to the shortage of available troops, Dalmatian hillmen and bandits were also hired or conscripted to serve the Romans against this threat. This further indicates just how serious this incursion was in Marcus's eyes.

Financially the war drained the Roman coffers, particularly due to the need to recruit more soldiers and hire mercenaries. However, rather than choosing what was likely the easiest option and increasing taxes which Marcus thought would have caused widespread problems, while still in Rome the Emperor held an auction in Trajan's Forum.[19] This choice of location was itself telling for such an event, reminding those present of Roman victories beyond the Danube, Marcus sold imperial property, everything from statues to candlesticks and clothing, in order to raise the money needed to continue the recruitment and hiring of forces to be sent north.[20] It is quite possible that Marcus did not feel particularly attached to the trappings of imperial wealth, as a Stoic and as a warrior emperor who spent most of his time on the frontiers fighting the enemies of the Empire, it seems unlikely that the selling these items proved to be much of a personal sacrifice. Marcus also offered to buy back anything bought at a later date, but didn't force anyone to sell anything they had purchased, making this appear somewhat like a very early version of a war bonds scheme where those who had access to the wealth were asked to invest in the war effort with the promise of recompense after the conclusion of the conflict.

Unfortunately, even these quite extreme measures were not sufficient to raise enough money to be able to afford to continue the war against the Germans, and Marcus was forced to debase the imperial currency. This was done by mixing non-precious metals with the precious metals that were used in the manufacture of the coinage. This would ensure that the same amount of precious metal could manufacture more coins but would lower the intrinsic value of the coin.

Meanwhile, after the major defeat suffered by the Roman forces across the Danube and very likely encouraged by signs of Roman weakness, another serious incursion occurred involving the Costoboci, a trans-Danubian tribe situated north of the relatively new province of Dacia, and the Sarmatians located west of Dacia. They crossed into Moesia raiding and pillaging as they went. They managed to advance all the way south into Macedonia and then into Greece, getting all the way to Eleusis, the home of the Eleusinian mysteries of Demeter near Athens. These invasions were very serious affairs and demonstrated that in its weakened state Rome was incapable of defending the entirety of the Danubian frontier or the nearby provinces. This vulnerability was pounced upon by a number of peoples, further compounding the problems faced by the Romans.

At the same time as the Costoboci and Sarmatians were mounting their attacks across the Danube, Dacia came under attack from Gothic tribes, leading to the death of Calpurnius Agrippa, the governor of two of the three Dacian provinces established under Hadrian. After the death of Agrippa, sometime in AD 169 Marcus placed the three Dacia provinces and Moesia Superior under the governorship of Marcus Claudius Fronto, who fought a number of successful battles against the invading Costoboci and Sarmatians before he too was killed in AD 170.[21]

At the same time as the Costoboci and Gothic incursions the Germans, buoyed by their major victory against the Roman forces that had been sent against them, crossed the Danube at a number of places and attacked Roman territory in force. This became a most serious incursion, with the Marcomanni and Quadi forces managing to destroy the Roman settlement of Opitergium and laying siege to the important Roman town of Aquileia. The fact that a major Roman settlement was being besieged by Germans caused alarm approaching panic, especially when Rome's past experience with the Germans is taken into account, with people thinking back to the invasions of the Cimbri and Teutones some two and a half centuries earlier.[22] That the Germans had made it well past the frontiers and even past the frontier provinces, and managed to besiege a Roman settlement located at the top of the Italian Peninsula so close to Rome significantly added to the urgency felt by those in Rome. However, Marcus was able to assemble sufficient forces and drive the barbarians back over the Danube.

Marcus rushed back to the front with his lieutenants Pertinax (who would later become emperor) and Pompeianus (who Marcus had rapidly married to his daughter, the widow of Lucius, before leaving Rome). Pompeianus was sent to Pannonia and tasked with expelling the Germans, taking Pertinax with him as one of his subordinate commanders. The process of driving the Germans out of Italy, the provinces and back across the Danube was time-consuming and difficult but ultimately successful. Together they inflicted heavy losses on the barbarian forces. Dio describes how Pertinax distinguished himself in these battles.[23]

Dio describes that when examining the corpses of the fallen the Romans discovered the bodies of armoured women amongst them. This would likely have been quite shocking for the Romans who would never have considered including women in their armies.[24] Their inclusion in the barbarian armies shows that this invasion most likely had settlement in Roman territory at the core of its purpose. Dio tells us that the army, having succeeded in pushing the invaders out of the Empire after a hard struggle, requested a donative from the Emperor to financially reward them for their efforts, however Marcus refused their request on the grounds that 'whatever they obtained over and above the regular amount would be rung from the blood of their parents and kinsmen',[25] further illustrating the dangerous position Rome found itself in at this time, and hinting at the fact that Marcus may have felt that the situation on the Danube was far from resolved. By AD 171 Marcus had based himself at Carnuntum, the Pannonian capital, and was receiving embassies from a variety of barbarian peoples. Carnuntum was the logical choice of base for an attack against the Danubian Germans, in particular the Marcomanni. His actions here, and the agreements he entered into at this time, go some way towards clarifying Marcus's strategy for the defeat of the trans-Danubian invaders. He engaged in peace talks with the Quadi and others, in an effort to break them from their alliance with the Marcomanni. As a part of the peace terms the Quadi had agreed to they were to present the Emperor with a great many horses and cattle, promising to return 13,000 captives to begin with. He sent the tribes, led by the twelve-year-old Battarius, against the Gothic chieftain Tarbus who had invaded Dacia, and gave them money in return for the promised alliance.

Marcus was trying to return affairs beyond the Danube to the way they had been previously by using the age-old Roman tactic of playing the various barbarian tribes off against each other. This was based on the idea that as individual tribes none of these barbarians, even the very numerous Marcomanni, posed an insurmountable threat to the Empire, but when unified, spreading discontent among neighbouring communities and demonstrating that Rome was weakened and vulnerable along the Danubian front, the threat posed could have spelt the end of the Empire. Marcus agreed to settle a substantial number of barbarians within the Empire, in Dacia, Moesia, Pannonia, provincial Germany and Italy itself. This policy proved problematic as those settled at Ravenna in Italy rose up and seized the city.[26] Marcus was forced to expel all of the barbarians he had settled in Italy. He learnt his lesson and never settled barbarians in Italy again.

The Emperor made use of the barbarians wherever possible to weaken other tribes in conflict with Rome. In one example, the Astingi, a northern people entered Dacia, led by their two chieftains Raus and Raptus accompanied by all their women and children, looking for somewhere to settle. They offered their help to Rome in exchange for money and land. The Astingi were sent against the Costoboci by Marcus, who was probably less concerned about who actually won than that both the barabarian tribes would be weakened. Although apparently successful, the Astingi attacked Dacia anyway and were defeated by yet another barbarian tribe, the Lacringi, who feared that the Astingi might attack them next. In the end Marcus gave money and land to the weakened Astingi. The Cotini also received aid from the Romans. In return they were to participate in the war against the Marcomanni, which when the time came they did not in fact do.

In AD 172 Marcus was able to reap the benefit of his extensive diplomatic manoeuvring and defeat the Marcomanni in battle, largely because they had lost the assistance of their allies the Quadi. This victory saw Marcus awarded the title *Germanicus* (Conqueror of the Germans) for the first time. When the Romans and the Marcomanni came to terms, the Germans were to hand over all hostages and traitors and any plunder that they had taken in Roman territory, and although they would be allowed to trade with Rome, this would be strictly monitored and controlled by Roman officials. Finally, they were required to stay 10 miles north of the Danube at all times.

The Emperor was determined to put an end to the Sarmatian threat along the Danube as well. Dio tells us that he attacked and defeated the Iazyges first on land and then on the Danube itself.[27] Because of the unique circumstances of the latter battle it is the most conscientiously described battle of Marcus's northern wars. The Romans chased the Iazyges onto the frozen surface of the Danube. The fleeing Sarmatians realizing that the Romans were pursuing them onto the ice, thought that the advantage had swung back to them, because the Roman forces had no experience fighting on a treacherous icy surface. The Sarmatians turned their horses, who had been trained to keep their footing on ice, and some charged at their Roman pursuers whilst others tried to outflank them. Far from panicking, the Romans formed into a tight formation with the legionaries facing in all directions, most of them throwing their shields onto the ice. The legionaries, placing one foot on the grounded shields, were able to minimize the adverse effects of the slippery surface. In this way they were able to receive the Sarmatian charge.

The Roman tactics in this battle saw them try to turn the engagement into a wrestling match. As the Iazyges approached the legionaries would grab at any part of the mounted warrior that they could, be it their shield or spearshaft, in an effort to drag them from their horses. When this failed they grabbed the horses' bridles and tried to pull down both horse and rider. When they managed to ground their foes, something the Sarmatians weren't accustomed to, the Romans would wrestle them, killing them at close quarters on the increasingly bloody ice using the advantage of their heavier armour to dominate their more lightly-equipped opponents. The Romans, according to Dio, literally resorted to using their feet and teeth when the enemy landed on them. Roman tenacity won through in the end, with very few of the Iazyges able to escape the slaughter.[28]

The Sarmatians sent envoys to Marcus asking for peace, but the Emperor refused to come to terms with the Iazyges because he planned to assault the Quadi, close allies of the Iazyges, and because he felt that they had not proven themselves trustworthy when it came to their negotiations with Rome. They had failed to return all captives as had been agreed in the earlier treaty and had in fact only returned those unfit to be sold or put to work. Marcus, having at least temporarily neutralized the Iazyges, launched a renewed attack on the Quadi in AD 173. He was deeply angered by the fact that they had changed kings without consulting him and to make matters worse they had apparently taken in Marcomanni fugitives whilst there was still a war being fought between Rome and the Marcomanni, a breach of the peace treaty between Rome and the Quadi.[29] The Quadi replaced their king Furtius, who had been appointed by Marcus, with Ariogaesus who was a member of an anti-Roman faction within the Quadi. Marcus was so incensed by the appointment of the new Quadi king that he placed a price on his head. A thousand gold pieces would be given to anyone who presented the Quadi king to the

Emperor alive, and 500 gold pieces would be given to anyone who presented his head to Marcus. This was a very uncommon emotional reaction from the Emperor and when the Quadi king was eventually handed over, he was not killed or abused in any way but sent into exile in Alexandria.

The war with the Quadi nearly ended very badly for the Romans. The vastly numerically superior Quadi managed to surround the Romans, who were forced to defend themselves from all sides. Fighting with great determination they managed to hold off the enemy. The Quadi abruptly stopped their assault, having determined that if they waited long enough and kept the Romans trapped where they were, the heat and thirst would in short order win their victory for them. To this end the Quadi stationed guards to prevent the Romans leaving but ceased attacking their enemy. The conditions were taking their effect on the Romans, who according to Dio were fatigued, wounded and dehydrated almost to the point of defeat when clouds suddenly gathered and a divinely-inspired heavy rain fell on the Romans.[30] According to Dio, Arnuphis, an Egyptian magician, invoked Mercury and various other deities to attract the rain, but Xiphilinus, the epitomiser of Dio's work, argues that the rain was the result of a entirely Christian legion, which Marcus at a loss for what to do turned to for help, praying for the rain.

The legionaries opened their mouths to the sky drinking the rain water as it fell, and the Quadi, seeing their plan ruined, attacked again. The Romans still far from sated drank and fought the barbarians at the same time. The sources indicate that the Romans might still have lost the engagement except that a violent thunder and hailstorm started, targeting only the Quadi and avoiding the Roman forces, if Dio is to be believed. The thunderbolts striking the Germans ignited oil in their midst which was spread further still by the pouring rain but did not touch the Romans, who were still quenching their thirst. The Quadi, seeing this, came to the conclusion that their only option was surrender to the Romans. Marcus accepted their surrender and took pity on them but in order to ensure their continued compliance he stationed 20,000 troops in forts in their territory and that of the Marcomanni.

Marcus Aurelius also came to terms with the Iazyges. The agreement reached gave the Iazyges access to Roman markets but only on specified days. It appears that at this stage the Iazyges were banned from travelling through Dacia to meet up with the related Roxolani tribe situated east of the province, indicating that the free communication and travel between the two Sarmatian tribes was a concern for the Romans, possibly because of the embryonic anti-Roman coalition evident in the early stages of the Dacian Wars and during the Marcomannic Wars. Additionally, like the Quadi the Iazyges were required to settle more than 10 miles away from the Danube. Marcus had apparently planned to destroy the Iazyges but was forced to restrain himself and set reasonable peace terms when Avidius Cassius, stationed in the East, declared himself emperor. The Marcomanni had also sent envoys to Marcus, requesting that they should have the neutral zone in their territory reduced to 5 miles from its current 10, especially as the Marcomanni had been faithful to the peace terms struck with Rome. The emperor granted them their request.

> And so by crushing the Marcomanni, the Sarmatians, the Vandals, and even the Quadi he freed Pannonia from bondage.
>
> HA. *Marcus* XVII.3.

Avidius Cassius, one of Marcus's most trusted and competent generals who had been placed in command in the East, apparently thinking the Marcus was dead declared himself emperor. Some sources suggest that Faustina, Marcus's wife, deciding that her husband would not survive much longer due to illness and realizing that Commodus was too young to assume the imperial purple, encouraged Cassius in his rebellion. This forced Marcus to leave matters on the Danube unfinished; he withdrew significant forces from this theatre and marched east to confront Cassius and his forces. The revolt lasted a mere three months. Cassius was killed and decapitated, his head being brought to Marcus who was still making his way east with the army.[31] The Emperor, we are told, refused to even look at the head of Cassius, his onetime friend, as he was not pleased by the killing. Marcus did not inflict harsh punishments against the communities that had sided with the pretender or even against Cassius's family. The rebel's sons were allowed to live and received a portion of their father's wealth, although they were sent into exile.

Cassius's actions had brought Marcus's momentum against the trans-Danubians to a halt. His departure for the East to deal with the rebellion occurred at the point when some believe Rome could have ended the northern threat with a decisive blow, but instead his hurried departure gave Rome's enemies the opportunity to rebuild their strength and regain their desire to attack Roman territory.

The Second Marcomannic War

Unfortunately, even less is known about the events of the years AD 178–180, the last of Marcus's principate and his life. In 178 after having been inducted into the Eleusinian mysteries whilst in Athens and having celebrated a triumph in Rome, Marcus was forced to return to the Danube. The two commanders who had been left in charge, although capable and experienced generals, were not able to keep matters under control. The archaeological evidence illustrates that Roman holdings in Pannonia were destroyed during this period. The extent of this destruction is, however, debatable with thirty-three demonstrable destructions difficult to precisely date and possibly belonging to either the first or second Northern war.

The Emperor, having performed the ritual of throwing a bloody spear into enemy territory in order to ensure the war was just in the eyes of the Gods, returned to the frontier with his son Commodus. The Emperor put a large army under the command of Paternus who was sent to fight the barbarians and after a day long battle which saw the barbarians destroyed, Marcus received his tenth salutation as *imperator*.

Envoys were sent to the Emperor from the Iazyges and the Buri. The Iazyges asked for the terms of the treaty reached earlier to be eased, a request the Emperor, keen to keep them onside, granted. One of the main concessions was that the Iazyges were now permitted to travel through Dacia so that they could undertake their seasonal migrations and communicate with their kin, the Roxolani. Marcus did place a condition on any travel through Dacia – the Iazyges were only allowed to travel through the province under the supervision of the Dacian governor. Both the Buri and the Iazyges sought assurances from Marcus that if they fought the Quadi with Rome that the war would be prosecuted to the end so that the Quadi would be unable to exact revenge later. The Quadi and Marcomanni came to the emperor to complain of the conduct of the troops he had stationed in their respective territories, saying that the troops would not allow them to sow their fields or graze their stock. Marcus appears to have continued with this policy as Dio tells us that the Quadi, angered by the garrisons in their territory, attempted to migrate into the lands of the Semnones, but the emperor, aware of their movements, sent troops to prevent them leaving. Thus the great philosopher-emperor Marcus Aurelius spent the remainder of his life making war on the Marcomanni, Hermunduri, Sarmatians and the Quadi,[32] before perishing due to illness in Pannonia in 180 AD

> If Marcus had lived longer, he would have subdued the entire region.
>
> Dio, LXXII.33.1

The opportunity to secure the Danube and achieve Marcus's ultimate objective was bequeathed to the emperor's only surviving son Commodus. The sources suggest that the new emperor quickly grew tired of the rigors of campaigning on the frontiers and, contrary to the advice he received from Marcus's most trusted advisers, he hastily concluded the Northern wars. The peace terms reached were described by Dio as 'not discredible' to Rome but the *Historia Augusta* described Commodus's peace as a submission to the enemy's terms, ending the Roman successes on the Danube.[33]

The reign of Marcus Aurelius had seen the development of a real crisis on the Danubian frontier. No longer were the peoples beyond the Danube held in check by Rome's aggression. Rome's heavy involvement on another frontier and an internal crisis caused by a plague brought back by troops returning from the East further weakened the Empire. The trans-Danubian peoples, encouraged by any apparent weakness, flooded across the Danube into Raetia, Noricum, Pannonia and through Dacia into Moesia. Internal crisis in Rome and external pressures beyond the frontier mounted and enhanced the nature of the crisis. Even though the Marcomanni, Quadi and Buri were made to accept terms with Rome by Commodus, these dangerous enemies were far from defeated and matters on this frontier were far from resolved with the continued growth of the external pressures that brought about these wars continued to develop over the coming years.

Conclusion:
'The Best Defence is a Good Offence'?

Now we switch from an Empire of gold to one of iron and rust.

Roman conquests along the volatile Danubian frontier happened over a period of approximately 150 years and under the command of numerous emperors and the best generals of their times, beginning with Octavian in 35 BC and ending with Trajan's conquest of Dacia in AD 107. At its greatest extent the Danubian frontier formed the northern boundary of Raetia, Noricum, Pannonia, Moesia and the southern boundary of Dacia. It was the setting for numerous battles, important victories and significant Roman losses. After Rome had completed its conquests along the Danube, this frontier stretched over 2,800km and formed the longest continuous natural border in continental Europe.

After the expansion of the Julio-Claudian emperors on the Danube, periodic attempts were made to strengthen the frontiers and deal with the threats posed by the peoples beyond them. Vespasian, Domitian, Trajan, Hadrian, and Marcus Aurelius all expended significant energy trying to subdue the Danubian threats but their efforts did not diminish them for more than a short period. A regressive, increasingly inward-looking mentality adopted by the Romans after Trajan's success in Dacia meant Rome was no longer the power to be feared beyond its frontiers.

Traditionally the frontier had only been limited by how far beyond the limits of the Empire Rome was willing to project its power and influence. However, a change in the Empire's mentality saw Roman limits become increasingly defined and significant pressure on the frontiers applied by people beyond them. This change to defined limits dramatically reduced the intimidation value of the limited Roman forces assigned to protect the periphery. When pressure from further north was applied to the Gothic peoples immediately north of the Danube, their fear of the new threat from the Huns exceeded their fear of Rome's reaction their movement into the Empire.

Additionally, Rome was not able to keep increasing the size of the military forces assigned to protect the frontiers. The expenses associated with the maintenance of the army had already proven an issue as far back as Augustus's principate when he halved the number of legions, from sixty to thirty, after the conclusion of the Civil War. In effect, the military strength required to prevent the ingress of the barbarians into the Empire just wasn't affordable. The shift to a defensive policy made matters worse and exacerbated the lack of manpower since a defensive policy, by its very nature, relies more heavily on troop numbers than an offensive policy. An aggressor is able to concentrate their available forces at a specific point, but a defensive policy relies on distributing troops across all possible weak points that an enemy might choose to attack.

The Danube remained a focal point till the fall of the Western Empire with numerous invasions, Dacia in particular standing proud of the rest of the Danubian provinces as the only province situated north of the Danube. It presented multiple fronts for aggressive neighbours. In the 260s the Empire started to lose control of regions not directly under Rome's control, and the region between the Rhine and Danube was settled by the German Alamanni. The Carpi, a free-Dacian tribe, invaded Dacia in AD 248–50, the Goths in 258, 263 and again in 267 and 269. In time the Emperor Aurelian (AD 270–5) judged the increased difficulty of retaining the province against continuous incursion too costly and withdrew from the province in 271 or 272. What had been Roman Dacia was settled by Sarmatians, Goths and free Dacians. The last imperial conquest became the first province lost less than 200 years after it was taken by Trajan: the Empire would never again control this region. Aurelian renamed parts of Moesia south of the Danube Dacia and resettled many displaced colonists there, possibly to minimize the loss of face associated with the withdrawal. The abandonment of trans-Danubian Dacia only eased the pressure on this frontier for a short time, delaying matters rather than resolving them.

In AD 334 Constantine was forced to fight the Sarmatians on this frontier. Apparently he also claimed a Dacian victory, demonstrated by his adoption of the honorific 'Dacicus Maximus' suggesting that he had re-established Trajan's Dacia which he clearly hadn't. Constantius too was forced to fight on the middle Danube for a number of years, and in AD 358 and 359 he led huge punitive campaigns against the Quadi and the Sarmatians, apparently eliminating the latter as a power on this frontier, which at first seemed beneficial to the Empire (his immediate successors had little trouble on the frontier), but time would see that the elimination of the Sarmatians permitted, if not fuelled, the growth of Gothic power in the region. The Gothic confederacy, which was made up of a number of kingdoms including Germans, Sarmatians, Dacians and Carpi, became a major force along the Danube and the Rhine. Increasingly pressure was applied to the Gothic peoples north of the Danube by the Huns and this pressure was in turn led to mounting pressure on the Danube that would eventually explode.

Large numbers of Goths started to petition for peaceful entry into the Empire, the response varying seemingly at random, at least that's how some of the Goths must have viewed the decisions. In AD 376 one large group of Goths, the Tervingi, was permitted entry into the Empire whilst another, the Greuthungi, were refused. Having allowed the Tervingi permission to peacefully enter the Empire, the Romans found that supplying and settling this people was much more difficult than they had anticipated, combined with the corruption of Roman officials who saw an opportunity to become wealthy at the expense of the starving Goths. The Roman officials assigned to the Goths, when supplies became scarce, rounded up as many dogs as they could find, selling them to the starving Goths at a cost of a slave per dog. To make matters worse the Romans attempted to assassinate the Gothic leaders at a banquet, leading to the battle of Adrianople in AD 378 where Rome lost two-thirds of the field army it had committed to the battle and the Emperor Valens. This loss was a severe shock to the Romans as everyone, probably including the Goths themselves, thought Rome would win. This critical defeat led to the overrunning of Thrace and Illyricum. This was a major defeat that had a significant psychological effect on the Empire after which we can see an increasing barbarianization of the Roman military and a shift to trying to dissuade Gothic raids and attacks by paying them off.

The Danube frontier posed a significant and largely continuous threat from the time Rome first encountered the peoples of the Danube. Many Roman soldiers fought and died on this frontier, the Empire was forced to garrison a very substantial part of its overall military manpower on this frontier and at times was forced to recruit slaves and bandits into the army in order to be able to maintain enough force on this frontier to protect it. In the end even these measures did not prove sufficient to maintain the integrity of the Danubian frontier, eventually leading to the fall of the Western Empire.

Notes

Chapter 1: Illyricum: The Push Towards the Danube

1. Polybius, II.2.
2. Badian, p. 75.
3. Polybius, II.2.4–6; Van Antwerp Fine, 29.
4. Polybius II.6.
5. Polybius, II.3.1.
6. Badian, 73.
7. Polybius, II.8.
8. Polybius, II.9.
9. Polybius, II.10.
10. Plutarch, *Themistocles* 14.
11. Polybius, II.10.
12. Polybius, II.3.
13. Ibid.
14. Polybius, II.3.7.
15. Polybius, II.4.6.
16. Polybius, II.4.7–9; Van Antwerp Fine, 29.
17. Polybius, II.8.
18. Polybius, II.8.12.
19. Polybius, II.8.13.
20. Polybius, II.9.
21. Polybius, II.9.3–6.
22. Polybius, II.9.7.
23. Badian, 77.
24. Polybius, II.11.3–4; Appian, X.II.8.
25. Polybius, II.11.8–13.
26. Badian, 78.
27. Polybius II.12.3–4; Appian, X.II.9.
28. Badian, 80.
29. Van Antwerp Fine, 30; Appian, X.II.9.
30. Badian, 82.
31. Van Antwerp Fine, 30.
32. Ibid., 28.

33. Wilkes, 163.
34. Badian, 87.
35. Ibid., 88.
36. Livy, xli.19.
37. Livy, xlii.52.
38. Herodotus, *The Persian Wars* II.167.
39. Webber, *The Gods of Battle*, 108.
40. See Figure 1 *sica*.
41. Webber, *Odrysian Cavalry Arms*, 530.
42. Polybius, 29.3.
43. Livy, 44.30.7.
44. Wilkes, 174.
45. Appian, *Ill* 9.
46. Livy, 44.31.
47. Wilkes, 189; Dzino, 40.
48. Polybius, XXXII.18.
49. Polybius,XXXII.13.13; XXXII.23.
50. Polybius, 32.23.
51. Appian, *Ill* X.II.11.
52. Polybius, XXXII.13.

Chapter 2: Julius Caesar

1. Appian *Ill* X.III.12.
2. Ibid.
3. Ibid.
4. Appian, *Ill* X.III.
5. Appian, *Ill* X.III.12.
6. Suetonius, 44.
7. Crişan, 80.
8. Ibid., 98.
9. Ibid., 80.
10. Jordanes, *Getica* XI.67.
11. Strabo, VII.3.13.
12. Strabo, VII.3.11.
13. Crişan, 98, 100.
14. Ibid., 105.
15. Ibid., 112.
16. Ibid.
17. Ibid., 87.
18. Ibid.
19. Ibid., 87–9.

20. Strabo, V.1.6; VII.3.11;52; Crişan, 114.
21. Strabo, VII.3.11.

Chapter 3: Octavian's Illyricum

1. Appian, *Ill* X.IV.16.
2. Appian, *Ill* X.IV.23.
3. Appian, *Ill* X.III.12.
4. Dio, XLVIII.29.2; Appian *Ill* IV.16.
5. Appian, *Ill* X.IV.18.
6. Dio, XLIX 34.2.
7. Iapydes is also spelled Iapodes and Iapudes.
8. Appian, *Ill* X.IV.18.
9. Appian *Ill* X.IV.
10. Dzino, 23–4.
11. Strabo, VII.5.4.
12. Strabo, IV.4.3.
13. Wilkes, 239.
14. Appian, *Ill* X.IV.20.
15. See Figure 1 *sica*.
16. See Figure 14 Decebalus's Suicide.
17. Wilkes, 235.
18. Ibid., 201.
19. Ibid.
20. Appian, *Ill* X.IV.16.
21. Appian, *Ill* X.IV.18.
22. Ibid.
23. Ibid.
24. Appian, *Ill* X.IV.19.
25. Ibid.
26. Dio, XLIX 35.2. mentions that the Metulians fortified their city and repulsed many assaults, burned many siege engines and injured Caesar himself.
27. Appian, *Ill* X.IV.19–21.
28. Appian, *Ill* X.IV.19.
29. Ibid.
30. Appian, *Ill* X.IV.20.
31. Appian, *Ill* X.IV.19.
32. Ibid.
33. Appian, *Ill* X.IV.21; Dio, XLIX.35.2.
34. Appian, *Ill* X.IV.21.
35. Appian, *Ill* X.IV.21.
36. Dio, XLIX.36.1.

37. Appian, *Ill* X.IV.23.
38. Dio, XLIX, 36.2.
39. Appian *Ill* X.IV.16: 18: 22, Dio XLIX.37.1.
40. Also known as Siscia in Dio, it is the site of modern-day Sisak.
41. Appian, *Ill* X.IV.23.
42. Appian, *Ill* X. IV.22ff.
43. Also Versus.
44. Appian, *Ill* X.V.26.
45. Appian, *Ill* X.V.26; Wilkes, 197.
46. Levick, *Augustus* 43.
47. Plutarch, *Antony* LXXXV.2–3; Dio, LI.10.6–LI.14.2.
48. Strauss, 190.
49. Livy, 39.35.
50. Dio, LI.24.4.
51. Dio, LI.23.3.
52. Dio, LI.24.3–4.
53. Dio, LI.25.4.
54. Dio, LI.26.1–3.
55. Dio, LI.26.5.
56. Dio, LI.26.6.
57. Dando-Collins, 212–16. The *spolia opima* (lit. 'rich spoils') was a trophy consisting of the enemy commander's arms and armour, awarded to a Roman general only if he had killed the commander in single combat.

Chapter 4: The Danube as the Northern Frontier

1. Dio LIV. 20.3.
2. Ibid.
3. Webber, 232, n. 1.
4. Levick, 237.
5. Livy, *History of Rome* 5.33.
6. Strabo, IV.6.6.
7. Dio, LI.22.2.
8. Powell, 56.
9. Velleius Paterculus, II.95.2.
10. Alfödy, xxii.
11. Strabo, IV.6.9.
12. Horace, *Odes* 1.16.
13. Alföldy, 44.
14. Strabo, VII.
15. Alföldy, 73.
16. Ibid., 52.

17. Appian, *Ill* 29.
18. Florus, II.22.
19. Appian, *Ill* 29.
20. Dio, LIV.20.2.
21. Alföldy, 55.
22. Strabo, IV.6.
23. Strabo, IV.20.
24. Seager, 20.
25. Ibid., 17, 20.
26. Dio, LIV.28.1.
27. Dio, LIV.29.1.
28. Velleius Paterculus, II.XCVI.2.
29. Velleius Paterculus, II.XCIX.
30. Velleius Paterculus, II.XCVI.2.
31. Lewis & Reinhold, Vol. 1, 581.
32. Dio, 54.36.2.
33. Florus, 2.20.f.; Augustus, *Res Gestae* 30; Tacitus *Annals* 4.44.
34. Syme, 400.
35. Dio, LIV.36.2.
36. Augustus, *Res Gestae* 30.
37. Florus, *Epitome* II, 28 = IV, 12.
38. Augustus, *Res Gestae* 30.
39. Strabo, VII.3.8.
40. Seager, 22; Dio, 55.2.1.
41. Seager, 23.

Chapter 5: The Pannonian Uprising of AD 6 to 9

 1. Seager, 23.
 2. Ibid., 32, 33.
 3. Suet., *Tib* 16.
 4. See map on page xvi – The Western Empire.
 5. See Chapters 3 and 4.
 6. Velleius Paterculus, II.110.
 7. Velleius Paterculus. II.96.3.
 8. Suet., *Tib* 16.
 9. Velleius Paterculus, II.111.1.
10. Seager, 33.
11. Velleius Paterculus, II.110.3.
12. Velleius Paterculus, II.110.6.
13. Velleius Paterculus, II.111.
14. Radman-Livaja and Dizdar, 48.

15. Dio, LV.30.
16. Dio, LV.32.
17. Dio, LV.31.
18. Ibid.
19. Dio, LV.34.3.
20. Dio, LV.31.
21. Dio, LV.33.
22. Ibid.
23. Seager, 35.
24. Dio, LVI.11.2.
25. Dio LVI.12.2–3.
26. Dio LVI.14.2–3.
27. Dio LVI.14.6–7.
28. Dio, LVI.14.7-8.
29. Dio, LVI.15.1; LXVIII.9.

Chapter 6: The Dacians: an Emerging Empire

1. Strabo, VII.3.2.
2. Oltean, 42.
3. One could argue that even Burebista's unification did not fulfil this criteria.
4. Strabo, VII.3.5.
5. Crişan, 102.
6. Oltean, 50.
7. Arnold, 160.
8. Oltean, 80.
9. Caesar, 7.23.
10. Ibid.
11. *Emplekton* was the filling in walls that could be made up of broken pottery, earth and rubble.
12. See the depiction of Costesti, Trajan's Column, Scene XXV.
13. Oltean, 110.
14. Hodges, 250.
15. Lockyer, 44.
16. Cioata.
17. Todd, 36.
18. See figures 5, 6 and 7.
19. More extensive arguments have been made regarding the *falx* actually looked like see Schmitz, *Digressus* and Schmitz, *Roman Annexation*.
20. Fronto, 9: 'In bellum profectus est cum cognitis militibus hostem Parthum contemnentibus, sagittarum ictus post ingentia Dacorum falcibus inlata vulnera despicatui habentibus'; cf. Sim, 37–40; Goldsworthy, 127.

21. Sim and Kaminski, 90.
22. See figures 5, 6 and 7.
23. Bishop argues that a *manica* with a reversed plate configuration would not have worked and would have significantly hindered movement.
24. The author undertook testing with a standard *manica* design and found that the *falx* was able to cut pass the plates into the flesh of the arm all the way to the bone which also sustained significant damage.
25. Trajan's Column, Scene LXVI, Cast 169.
26. Trajan's Column, Scene XL, Cast 104.
27. Dio LXVIII.9; Rossi, 125.
28. Trajan's Column, Scene XXV, Cast 63; Lepper and Frere, 272.
29. Strabo, VII.3.13.
30. Trajan's Column, Scene XXXI – XLI.
31. Strobel, 61.
32. Roman Imperial Coin 98a; RIC 147.

Chapter 7: The Flavian Danube

1. Tac., *Hist* 1.79.
2. Ibid.
3. Suet., *Vesp* 4.
4. Suet., *Vesp* 3.
5. Levick, *Vespasian* 1.
6. Suet., *Vesp* 6.
7. Grumeza, 155.
8. Tac., *Hist* 3.46.
9. Ibid.
10. Pitassi, 253.
11. Suet., *Vesp* 2.
12. Dio., LXVI.18.
13. Jones, 127.
14. Tac., *Agric* 39.
15. Frontinus, I.3.
16. Suet., *Dom* 6.
17. Wilcox, Trevino and McBride, 28.
18. See map on page xvii – Thrace.
19. Jones, 132.
20. Ibid.
21. Suet., *Dom* 6.
22. Wilcox, Trevino and McBride, 28.
23. Strabo, VII.3.13.
24. Dio, LXVII.6.3.

25. Dio. LXVII.6; Schmitz, *Roman Annexation* 163; Syme, *The Lower Danube under Trajan* 31; Strobel, 155.
26. Jones, 136.
27. Dio, LXVIII.
28. Frontinus, 1.1.8.
29. Ibid., 2.11.7.
30. Juvenal 4.144–146.
31. Tac., *Hist* 2.86, 3.50.
32. Suet., *Dom* 6.1.
33. Ibid.
34. Dio, LXVII.6.
35. Jones, 141.
36. Jordanes, *Getica* 77.
37. Ibid. 76.
38. Tac., *Hist* 1.79, 2.85.
39. Dio, LXVII.10.1.
40. Jones, 142.
41. Tac., *Germ* 30.3.
42. Dio, LXVII.7.1.I.
43. Suet., *Dom* 6.1.
44. Tac., *Hist* 1.2.
45. Pliny, *Panegyricus*.
46. Jones, 133.

Chapter 8: Trajan's Dacian Wars

1. Pliny, *Panegyricus* 6.3; 8.5; Bennett, 44.
 2. Bennett, 46.
 3. Ibid., 50.
 4. Ibid., 52.
 5. See figures 5, 6 and 7 – Adamklissi older armour.
 6. Dio LXVIII.15.6.1–3.
 7. Strobel, 8.
 8. Oltean, 50.
 9. Bennett, 89.
10. Ibid.
11. Sasel.
12. Trajan's Column Scene XXXIV.
13. Bennett, 127.
14. Dio, LXVII.6.
15. Davies, 74; Lepper and Frere, 91–4.

16. The fact that there is no engagement between the Romans and Dacians on the Column until the battle of Tapae (Trajan's Column Scene XXIV) indicates that the Dacians had abandoned the lowlands.
17. Schmitz, *Roman Annexation* 100.
18. Ibid., 102.
19. Dio, LXVIII.8.
20. Battle of the Bandages, Trajan's Column Scene XXIX–XLV; Dio LXVIII.8.
21. Trajan's Column Scene XXV.
22. Ibid.
23. Crişan, 89.
24. Trajan's Column Scene XXXVIII.
25. Crişan, 194.
26. Trajan's Column Scene CXIV.
27. Arrian, 1.3–4.
28. Trajan's Column Scene CXIV.
29. Trajan's Column Scene XXXVII–XXXIX.
30. Trajan's Column Scene LIX.
31. Trajan's Column Scene LXIII–LXIV.
32. Trajan's Column Scene LXVI.
33. Bennett, 29.
34. Dio, LXVIII.9.
35. Ibid.
36. Dio, LXVIII.10.3.

Chapter 9: Hadrian

1. *Historia Augusta* (HA), *Hadrian* 3.6.
2. HA, *Hadrian* 3.2., Barrett, 157.
3. Birley, *Hadrian* 156–7.
4. HA, *Hadrian* 3.9.
5. Ibid., 3.10.
6. Dio, LXVIII.17.1.
7. Birley, *Hadrian* 84.
8. Ibid., 163.
9. See above.
10. Mocsy, 87, 102–3, 193; Lepper and Frere, 309; Dio, LXVIII.10.3.
11. Mocsy, 193.
12. Ibid.
13. HA, *Hadrian* 6.8.
14. Bennett, 203.
15. Birley, *Hadrian* 85.

16. Ibid., 90–1.
17. Ibid., 166–8.

Chapter 10: The War of Many Nations

1. HA, *Marcus* 22.1 & 22.7.
2. Ibid., 24.5, 27.10.
3. Birley, *Marcus Aurelius* 176.
4. Ibid., 149ff.
5. HA, *Marcus* 14.1.
6. Birley, *Marcus Aurelius* 149.
7. HA, *Marcus* XXII.7.
8. *The Roman Army in Pannonia* 224.
9. Burns, *Rome and the Barbarians* 231.
10. Dio, LXXII.11.1.
11. Ibid.
12. Ibid.
13. Birley, *Marcus Aurelius* 155.
14. Ibid., 156.
15. Kovacs, 212.
16. Birley, *Marcus Aurelius* 159–60.
17. HA, *Marcus* XXIII.5.
18. Polyb., 3.117; Livy, 22.49.15.
19. Birley, *Marcus Aurelius* 160.
20. Ibid.
21. Ibid., 161.
22. HA, *Marcus* 21.6.
23. Dio, LXII 3.
24. Ibid., 3.3.
25. Ibid., 3.3–4.
26. Birley, *Marcus Aurelius* 170.
27. Dio, LXXII 12.7.
28. Ibid.
29. Dio, LXXI (I) 12.3; 13.2.
30. Dio, LXXII.14.8.
31. Birley, *Marcus Aurelius* 189.
32. HA, *Marcus* 27.10.
33. Dio LXXIII.1–3; HA, *Commodus* 3.

Select Bibliography

Alföldy, G., *Noricum*, Routledge, 2015.

Appian, trans. Horace White, *Roman History*, Vol. 2, Harvard UP, 1912.

Arnold, W.T., *The Roman System of Provincial Administration to the Accession of Constantine the Great*, MacMillan and Co. 1879.

Augustus, *Res Gestae Divi Augusti*, trans. P.A. Brunt and J.M. Moore, Oxford UP, 1986.

Badian, E., 'Notes on the Roman Policy in Illyria (230-201BC)', *Papers of the British School at Rome* Vol. 20 (1952), pp. 72–93.

Barrett, A. (ed.), *Lives of the Caesars*, Wiley, 2009.

Beckmann, M., *The Column of Marcus Aurelius: The Genesis & Meaning of a Roman Imperial Monument*, University of North Carolina, 2011.

Bennett, J., *Trajan Optimus Princeps*, Routledge, 2001.

Birley, A., *Hadrian: The Restless Emperor*, Routledge, 2000.

Birley, A., *Lives of the Caesars: The First Part of the Augustan History, with Newly Compiled Lives of Nerva and Trajan*, Penguin, 1982.

Birley, A., *Marcus Aurelius, a Biography*, Routledge, 1966.

Burns, T.S., *Rome and the Barbarians 100 BC – AD 400*, John Hopkins UP, 2009.

Caesar, *The Gallic War*, trans. H.J. Edwards, Harvard UP, 1970.

Cassius, Dio Cocceianus, *Dio Cassius Roman History*, trans. Cary Earnest and Foster Herbert Baldwin, Harvard UP, 1917.

Cassius, Dio Cocceianus, *Dio Roman History*, trans. Cary Earnest and Foster Herbert Baldwin, Harvard UP, 1924.

Cioata, D., *Warriors and Weapons in Dacia in the 2nd BC – 1st AD Centuries*, unpublished thesis, Universitatea Babeş-Bolyai, 2010.

Crişan, I.H., *Burebista and his Time*, Editura Academiei Republicii Socialiste Romania, 1978.

Dando-Collins, S., *Legions of Rome: The Definitive History of Every Imperial Roman Legion*, Quercus, 2010.

Davies, G.A.T., 'Trajan's First Dacian War', *The Journal of Roman Studies* 7 (1917), pp. 74–97.

Dzino, D., *Illyricum in Roman Politics, 229 BC-AD 68*, Cambridge UP, 2010.

Ferris, I.M., *Hate and War: The Column of Marcus Aurelius in Rome*, The History Press, 2009.

Florus, Lucius Anneus, and Cornelius Nepos, *Epitome of Roman History*, Harvard UP, 1929.

Frontinus, *Stratagems. Aqueducts of Rome*, trans. M.B. McElwain, Harvard UP, 1925.

Garnsey, P., and Saller, R.P., *The Roman Empire: Economy, Society, and Culture*, Duckworth, 1987.

Goldsworthy, A. *Roman Warfare*, Weidenfeld & Nicolson, 2000.

Grumeza, I., *Dacia*, University Press of America, 2009.

Hanson, W. S., Allason-Jones, L., and Breeze, D.J., *The Army and Frontiers of Rome: Papers Offered to David J. Breeze on the Occasion of His Sixty-fifth Birthday and His Retirement from Historic Scotland*, Journal of Roman Archaeology, 2009.

Herodotus, *The Persian Wars*, trans. A.D. Godley, Harvard UP, 1920.

Historia Augusta, Vol. I., trans. D. Magie, Harvard UP, 1932.

Hodges, H., *Technology in the Ancient World*, Barnes and Noble, 1992.

Horace, *Odes and Epodes*, trans. N. Rudd, Harvard UP, 2004.

Jones, B., *The Emperor Domitian*, Taylor and Francis, 2002.

Jordanes, *The Gothic History (Getica)*, trans. Dr. C.C. Mierow, Princeton UP, 1915.

Juvenal, *The Sixteen Satires*, trans. P. Green. London: Penguin Books, 1974.

Kovacs, P., *Marcus Aurelius' Rain Miracle and the Marcomannic Wars*, Brill, 2009.

Lepper, F., and Frere, S., *Trajan's Column, A New Edition of the Cichorius Plates: Introduction, Commentary and Notes*, Alan Sutton, 1988.

Levick, B., *Vespasian*, Routledge, 1999.

Levick, B., *The Government of the Roman Empire: A Sourcebook*, Routledge, 2000.

Levick, B., *Augustus, Image and Substance*, Taylor and Francis, 2014.

Lewis, N., and Reinhold, M., *Roman Civilization*, volume 1, Columbia UP, 1990.

Livy, *History of Rome (Ab Urbe Condita)*, Vol. 1, trans. B.O. Foster, Harvard UP, 1919.

Livy, *History of Rome (Ab Urbe Condita)*, Vol. 2, trans. B.O. Foster, Harvard UP, 1922.

Livy, *History of Rome (Ab Urbe Condita)*, Vol. 3, trans. B.O. Foster, Harvard UP, 1924.

Livy, *History of Rome (Ab Urbe Condita)*, Vol. 4, trans. B.O. Foster, Harvard UP, 1926.

Lockyer, K., 'The Late Iron Age Background to Roman Dacia: Some Considerations', in Hanson, W.S., and Haynes, I.P. (eds.), *Roman Dacia: The Making of a Provincial Society*, Journal of Roman Archaeology, 2004.

Luttwak, E., *The Grand Strategy of the Roman Empire: From the First Century AD to the Third*, Johns Hopkins UP, 1979.

Millar, F., *The Roman Empire and Its Neighbours*, Duckworth, 1981.

Morillo, C.A., Hanel, N., and Hernandez, E.M., *Limes XX*, Consejo Superior De Investigaciones Cientificas, 2009.

Mocsy, A., *Pannonia and Upper Moesia: A History of the Middle Danube Provinces of the Roman Empire*, Routledge & Keegan Paul, 1974.

Oltean, I.A., *Dacia: Landscape, Colonisation and Romanisation*, Routledge, Taylor & Francis Group, 2010.

Pitassi, M., *Navies of Rome* Boydell & Brewer, 2009.

Pliny, *Letters and Panegyricus* trans. B. Radice, Harvard UP, 1969.

Plutarch, *Lives* Vol. II, trans. B. Perrin, Harvard UP, 1914.

Plutarch, *Lives* Vol. IX, trans. B. Perrin, Harvard UP, 1920.

Polybius, *The Histories* Vol. 1, trans. W.R. Paton, Harvard UP, 1922.

Polybius, *The Histories* Vol. 2, trans. W.R. Paton, Harvard UP, 1922.

Polybius, *The Histories* Vol. 3, trans. W.R. Paton, Harvard UP, 1923.

Polybius, *The Histories* Vol. 4, trans. W.R. Paton, Harvard UP, 1925.

Polybius, *The Histories* Vol. 5, trans. W.R. Paton, Harvard UP, 1926.

Polybius, *The Histories* Vol. 6, trans. W.R. Paton, Harvard UP, 1927.

Powell, L., *Eager for Glory: The Untold Story of Drusus the Elder, Conqueror of Germania*, Pen & Sword Books, 2011.

Radman-Livaja, I., and Dizdar, M., *Archaeological traces of the Pannonian revolt 6 to 9 AD: evidence and conjectures*, Aschendorff Verlag, 2010.

Rossi, L., *Trajan's Column and the Dacian Wars*, Thames and Hudson, 1971.

Sasel, J., 'Trajan's Canal at the Iron Gate', *Journal of Roman Studies* 63 (1973), pp. 79–82.

Schmitz, M., *The Dacian Threat, 101-106 AD*, Caeros, 2005.

Schmitz, M., *Roman Annexation: Costs and Benefits of Trajan's Dacian Conquest*, VDM Verlag Dr. Muller, 2010.

Schmitz, M., 'Dacian Military Equipment and Technology', *Digressus* 11 (2011), pp. 1–30.

Seager, R., *Tiberius*, Wiley-Blackwell, 2005.

Sim, D., 'The Making and Testing of the Battle Falx Also Known as the Dacian Battle Scythe', *The Journal of Roman Military Equipment Studies* 11 (2000), pp. 37–40.

Sim, D., and Kaminski, J., *Roman Imperial Armour: The production of early imperial military armour*, Oxbow, 2011.

Strabo, *The Geography of Strabo*, trans. H.L. Jones. Vol. 3, Harvard UP, 1969.

Strauss, Barry, *The Spartacus War*, Weidenfeld and Nicolson, 2009.

Strobel, K., *Untersuchungen Zu Den Dakerkriegen Trajans: Studien Zur Geschichte Des Mittleren Und Unteren Donauraumes in der Hohen Kaiserzeit*, Dr Rudolf Habelt GMBH, 1984.

Suetonius, *The Twelve Caesars*, trans. R. Graves and M. Grant, Penguin, 1979.

Syme, R., 'The Lower Danube under Trajan', *The Journal of Roman Studies* 49 (1959), pp. 26–33.

Syme, R., *The Roman Revolution* Oxford UP, 2002.

Tacitus, C., *The Annals* Harvard UP, 1937.

Tacitus, Publius Cornelius, *Germania*, trans. W.H. Benario, Aris & Phillips, 1999.

Talbert, R., *Barrington Atlas of the Greek and Roman World*, Princeton UP, 2000.

Todd, M., *The Northern Barbarians 100 B.C. - A.D. 300*, Hutchinson & Co. Ltd, 1975.

Van Antwerp Fine, J., 'Macedon, Illyria and Rome 220-219 BC', *Journal of Roman Studies* Vol. 26 Part 1 (1936), pp. 24–39.

Visy, Zsot, *The Roman Army in Pannonia: An Archaeological Guide of the Ripa Pannonica*, Teleki Laszlo Foundation, 2003.

Webber, C., *The Gods of Battle: The Thracians at War, 1500 BC - AD 150*, Pen & Sword Military, 2011.

Wilcox, P., Trevino, R., McBride, A., and Embelton, G., *Barbarians against Rome: Rome's Celtic, Germanic, Spanish and Gallic Enemies*, Osprey History, 2000.

Wilkes, J.J., *The Illyrians*, Blackwell, 1995.

Index